BUSH-WHACKED

BUSH-WHACKED

CHRONICLES OF GOVERNMENT STUPIDITY

LELAND GREGORY

**Andrews McMeel
Publishing**

Kansas City

BUSH-WHACKED

05 06 07 08 09 RR2 10 9 8 7 6 5 4 3 2 1

ISBN-13: 978-0-7407-5471-5
ISBN-10: 0-7407-5471-8

Library of Congress Control Number: 2005921771

www.andrewsmcmeel.com

Book design by Diane Marsh

ATTENTION: SCHOOLS AND BUSINESSES

Andrews McMeel books are available at quantity discounts
with bulk purchase for educational, business, or sales promo-
tional use. For information, please write to: Special Sales
Department, Andrews McMeel Publishing, 4520 Main Street,
Kansas City, Missouri 64111.

BUSH-WHACKED

"**Y**ou've got to be able to speak clearly
in order to make this world a more peaceful place."
—*George W. Bush, Springfield, Ohio, September 27, 2004*

"**I** think it's very important for the American President
to mean what he says. That's why I understand
that the enemy could misread what I say.
That's why I try to be as clearly I can."
—*George W. Bush, Washington, D.C., September 23, 2004*

"**W**hat the country needs is a leader who speaks clearly."
—*George W. Bush, Kalamazoo, Michigan, May 3, 2004*

IRAQ, YOU BREAK

"**I** was proud the other day when both Republicans and Democrats stood with me in the Rose Garden to announce their support for a clear statement of purpose: you disarm, or we will."
—*George W. Bush, Manchester, New Hampshire, October 5, 2002*

ACCORDING TO THE UNITED STATES DEPARTMENT OF AGRICULTURE (USDA), AS OF 2004, "BATTER-COATED FRENCH FRIES ARE A FRESH VEGETABLE." SINCE THE REAGAN ADMINISTRATION CLASSIFIED KETCHUP AS A VEGETABLE IN 1981, OUR KIDS ARE FINALLY EATING HEALTHY.

AS GOD IS MY WITNESS

When born-again Christian George W. Bush announced his "faith-based" charity initiative to give federal tax dollars to church-based charities, many religious leaders denounced the idea. One of the most outspoken opponents was TV evangelist Pat Robertson, founder of the Christian Coalition, and an old friend of the Bush family. Church-based charities "will begin to be nurtured, if I can use that term, on federal money, and then they can't get off of it," Robertson prophesied. "It'll be like a narcotic; they can't then free themselves later on." From the first $30 million in grants, $500,000 went to Operation Blessing International of Virginia Beach, Virginia, which Pat Robertson founded and of which he still remains chairman. If Pat likens federal grant money to a narcotic, then he's got a half-million-dollar monkey on his back.

"It's not a dictatorship in Washington, but I tried to make it one in that instance."

—*George W. Bush, New Orleans, Louisiana, January 15, 2004, describing his executive order making faith-based charities eligible for federal subsidies. The executive order was made law on June 1, 2004.*

A BROAD MISTAKE

"**I** want to thank members of my administration who are here who will be involved in the implementation of some of the initiatives that I've outlined to the United States Congress. The Secretary of Education is here, Rod Paige, behind me. John Ashcroft is here. . . . And, most importantly, Alma Powell, secretary of Colin Powell, is with us. [Applause] She's kind of like my mother in many ways; she's always telling me what to do. [Laughter] And I'm always listening."

—*George W. Bush, Washington, D.C., January 30, 2003*

But apparently George wasn't listening very well. Alma Powell is Colin Powell's wife, not his secretary. What does he think this is, the Clinton administration?

CANADIAN PRIME MINISTER DOESN'T THINK BUSH IS "A MORON"
—*Reuters headline, November 21, 2002*

HIGH-FLYING FUNDING

It's called the Academic Center for Aging Aircraft, but it's not a place where old planes go to learn new tricks. It's a $4.2 million program, funded with taxpayer money, coordinated among the University of Dayton Research Institute, the Texas Engineering Experiment Station, and Georgia Tech Research Institute. Their mission is to help the Department of Defense develop, test, and implement new technologies for the maintenance and repair of aging aircraft. Basically, it's a very expensive program so college folks can come up with new ways of fixing old, useless, outdated airplanes. One day I hope someone comes up with a way to fix old, useless, outdated congressmen and their pork barrel projects.

"It's important for people to know that I'm the President of everybody."
—*George W. Bush, aboard* Air Force One,
January 14, 2005

BUSH-WHACKED

"I AM THE MASTER OF LOW EXPECTATIONS."

—*George W. Bush, aboard* Air Force One, *June 4, 2003*

SIGN OF THE TIMES

It's an image I'm sure most of us remember: a U.S. Navy S-3B Viking landing on the USS *Abraham Lincoln* and President Bush, complete with flight gear, springing out of the cockpit. What most don't know is that the President's advance team ordered the ship to turn around so the San Diego skyline didn't ruin the President's tailhook landing, the plane was custom-painted with Navy I and "George W. Bush Commander in Chief," the plane took two flybys over the aircraft carrier for dramatic effect, the justification for using the $27 million aircraft was that the ship was too far from shore to use a helicopter, and finally, there was a huge sign already on the carrier that read MISSION ACCOMPLISHED. It was the sign that made many people realize this wasn't a spontaneous event, but the biggest mystery is—who put up the sign and why was it there? The President says the Navy did it; the Navy says the White House did it. The White House said the sign was to signify the end of a tour of duty for the ship, the Navy said the sign was there for the President's visit. So which was it? We may never know. Nearly four months after "Sign-gate," on October 28, 2003, the President was still being dogged by the press for an explanation. He said, "The MISSION ACCOMPLISHED sign, of course, was put up by the members of the USS *Abraham Lincoln,* saying that their mission was accomplished. I know it was attributed somehow to some

ingenious advance man from my staff—they weren't that ingenious, by the way." On the other hand, White House press secretary Scott McClellan told CNN that in preparing the spontaneous visit from the President, the Navy wanted a MISSION ACCOMPLISHED banner, the White House agreed to create it, but the Navy actually put it up. We might never know who created the sign but the message is certainly clear: keep shuffling the blame, and eventually people forget. But those photographs will live on forever. MISSION ACCOMPLISHED!

POLL SHOWS VOTERS PREFER BUSH AT BARBECUE
—Associated Press headline, May 26, 2004

IN THE FISCAL YEAR 2005
FEDERAL BUDGET:

$1 MILLION

EARMARKED FOR THE STATE
HISTORICAL SOCIETY OF IOWA
IN DES MOINES, FOR THE
DEVELOPMENT OF EXHIBITS FOR
THE WORLD FOOD PRIZE.

IN THE DOG HOUSE

Since the attacks on the United States on September 11, 2001, several roads near the Pentagon have been closed to commercial traffic because of the fear of truck bombs. So when police saw a twenty-seven-foot-long vehicle cruising on the road they jumped into action. The two occupants of the car were detained and questioned by police before eventually being released. Police were immediately suspicious of the vehicle not only because it was on a restricted road but also because it was shaped like a hot dog. Yep, it was the famous Oscar Mayer Wienermobile, which had gotten lost while traveling through Washington on a yearlong charity drive. "[The drivers of the Wienermobile] were very apologetic," an Oscar Mayer spokeswoman said. "They just did not realize. They were sorry for any sort of traffic delay." Virginia State Police spokeswoman Lucy Caldwell said: "Obviously, this was a mistake. This hot dog posed no threat to us." However, a jar of mustard and some suspicious pickle relish were confiscated, and Dick Cheney was immediately taken to an undisclosed location.

"I like the idea of people running for office.
There's a positive effect when you run for office.
Maybe some will run for office and say, vote for me,
I look forward to blowing up America. I don't know,
I don't know if that will be their platform or not.
But it's——I don't think so. I think people who
generally run for office say, vote for me,
I'm looking forward to fixing your potholes,
or making sure you got bread on the table."

—*George W. Bush, Washington, D.C., March 16, 2005*

ANNOYING FEEDBACK

Not knowing their microphones were still on, George W. Bush and his running mate, Dick Cheney, on stage for a Labor Day campaign event in Naperville, Illinois, were caught saying:

GEORGE W. BUSH: There's Adam Clymer, major league a—hole from the *New York Times*.

DICK CHENEY: Yeah, big time.

—September 4, 2000

Pundits feared this remark would lose the Republicans the a—hole vote—but apparently they were wrong.

"And the time is getting worse. That's what people have got to understand up there in Washington or over there in Washington down there in Washington, whatever. Thought I was in Crawford for a minute."
—George W. Bush, Scranton, Pennsylvania, January 16, 2003

BUSH-WHACKED

MAY I SEE YOUR FAKE ID, PLEASE?

The *Milwaukee Journal Sentinel* conducted an investigation in March 2003 and uncovered the policy of the Social Security Administration for dealing with those who present fake identification in order to obtain a Social Security card. Employees were told if someone attempted to use an obviously phony ID, the ID was to be returned and the person would be asked to leave the building: no report was to be filed, no information on the person retained, and law enforcement was not to be called. Well, that certainly is Social but I don't know about the Security part.

"I think war is a dangerous place."
—*George W. Bush, Washington, D.C., May 7, 2003*

FROM THE MOUTHS OF BABES

During a press event to celebrate the signing of the Adoption Promotion Act of 2003, President Bush had Christopher and Diana Martin and their seven children with him in the Roosevelt Room at the White House. The act renews tax credits for adoptions and encourages families to find homes for more than five hundred thousand children in foster care. It's a great piece of legislation and truly worthy of a photo op of the President with a family filled with adopted children. Well, the President should have remembered never to work with kids because during his speech he mentioned that the children were adopted when they were six, eight, ten, and eleven years old.

BUSH: How old are you? (he asked Terrance Martin, the youngest child)

TERRANCE: Seven.

BUSH: Okay, seven. [Laughter] I'll take it up with the fact checker. Children who, at one time, were six, eight, ten, and eleven. [Laughter]

—*Signing of the Adoption Promotion Act of 2003, December 2, 2003*

IN THE FISCAL YEAR 2005 FEDERAL BUDGET: $25,000 FOR THE CLARK COUNTY (NEVADA) SCHOOL DISTRICT FOR CURRICULUM DEVELOPMENT TO STUDY MARIACHI MUSIC.

EGG ON HIS FACE

For the 2001 annual White House Easter Egg Roll on the South Lawn, the children got an extra surprise from the Secret Service. Printed on the back of the official egg roll ticket was a list of prohibited items the kiddies weren't allowed to bring including; aerosols of any kind, fireworks/firecrackers, animals (except guide dogs), food of any kind, backpacks (oversized), guns/ammunition, balloons, knives with blades over three inches, beverages of any kind, mace, chewing gum, nunchucks, duffle bags/suitcases, electric stun guns, and to make sure the kids didn't stunt their growth the ticket stressed that "smoking is not allowed."

"The war on terror involves Saddam Hussein because of the nature of Saddam Hussein, the history of Saddam Hussein and his willingness to terrorize himself."

—*George W. Bush, Grand Rapids, Michigan, January 29, 2003*

I DID NOT KNOW THAT

"**R**eports that say that something hasn't happened are always interesting to me, because as we know, there are known knowns; there are things we know we know. We also know there are known unknowns; that is to say we know there are some things we do not know. But there are also unknown unknowns, the ones we don't know we don't know. And if one looks throughout the history of our country and other free countries, it is the latter category that tend to be the difficult ones."

—*Secretary of Defense Donald Rumsfeld,*
DOD Press Briefing, February 12, 2002

MAN ARRESTED FOR DUMPING DIRT IN A FOREST

—*Associated Press headline dispatched from*
Coeur d'Alene, Idaho, November 2004 (Federal law prohibits
dumping anything on federal land, even soil.)

DO THESE PANTS MAKE
MY BUTT LOOK BIG?

United States Border Patrol officers are upset about their new uniforms. It's not that they're not fashionable or difficult to accessorize; it's that they're made in Mexico. A spokesman for Customs and Border Protection, now under the control of the Department of Homeland Security, complained that the uniforms, although purchased from a U.S. vendor, included work outsourced to other countries. "Sometimes, certain plants will do the cutting and send it off to other plants for assembling," said spokesman Jim Mitchie, in June 2004. "So, what's going on where, I can't tell you." As long as they don't mix stripes with polka dots or wear white shoes after Labor Day, I think everything will be fine.

"You're free. And freedom is beautiful. And, you know, it'll take time to restore chaos and order— order out of chaos. But we will."
—*George W. Bush, Washington, D.C., April 13, 2003*

REAL POLITICAL DOUBLESPEAK

On December 20, 2004, President Bush took talking to oneself to a new extreme: he promised he would not negotiate with himself in public. While at a televised news conference, the President was asked a question on the future of Social Security that he obviously didn't want to answer, so here's how he answered it:

"Now, the temptation is going to be, by well-meaning people such as yourself and others here, as we run up to the issue, to get me to negotiate with myself in public. To say, you know, 'What's this mean, Mr. President? What's that mean?' I'm not going to do that. I don't get to write the law. I'll propose a solution at the appropriate time."

***

"My six years as governor of Texas have been invaluable to me as I carry out my duties as the presidency."
—*George W. Bush, Washington, D.C., February 27, 2005*

THE ONLY PROBLEM WITH THIS QUOTE IS THAT GEORGE BUSH IS THE PRESIDENT, NOT THE PRESIDENCY.

I'M READY FOR MY CLOSE-UP . . .

In order to teach government employees how to respond to Freedom of Information Act (FOIA) requests, the U.S. Department of Defense (DOD), created a video in 2004 called *The People's Right to Know.* But when the Associated Press filed a FOIA request for a copy of the $70,500 video, it took the DOD a year and a half to release it because the Pentagon had to censor it first. Said Army lawyer Suzanne Council, "We couldn't get approval" from the owners of a number of movie clips used in the video. "We did our darnedest." The FOIA grants the government permission to censor or remove sensitive information, but there is no provision for removing copyrighted material. They should change the name of the video from *The People's Right to Know* to *The People's Rights?—No!*

"So one of my visits—one of the reasons I'm visiting here is to ask the question to people. Because if there's— moving too slow, or people are saying one thing and the other thing is not happening, now is the time to find out."

—*George W. Bush, Pierce City, Missouri, May 13, 2003*

I DIDN'T GET TIME TO REHEARSE MY SPONTANEOUS RESPONSE

REPORTER: In the last campaign, you were asked a question about the biggest mistake you'd made in your life, and you used to like to joke that it was trading Sammy Sosa. You've looked back before 9/11 for what mistakes might have been made. After 9/11, what would your biggest mistake be, would you say, and what lessons have you learned from it?

BUSH: I wish you would have given me this written question ahead of time, so I could plan for it. John, I'm sure historians will look back and say, gosh, he could have done it better this way, or that way. You know, I just—I'm sure something will pop into my head here in the midst of this press conference, with all the pressure of trying to come up with an answer, but it hasn't yet.

—*Prime Time Press Conference, Washington, D.C., April 13, 2004*

The FDA, which approved the relabeling of prunes to "dried plums," has drawn the line at prune juice being called "dried fruit juice" and won't allow it (because juice can't be dry, see). So it's still prune juice.

—*February 6, 2001*

I'M GOING TO DISNEY WORLD!

Florida Governor Jeb Bush (George Bush's younger brother) pledged $200,000 of state money to help local residents fight an infestation of mice in Orange County—the home of Disney World. Disney's public relations department responded to the report (and all the Mickey Mouse jokes) stating that the outbreak was near Apopka, miles from the mousetrap, uh, tourist trap, Disney World.

"Now, we talked to Joan Hanover. She and her husband, George, were visiting with us. They are near retirement— retiring—in the process of retiring, meaning they're very smart, active, capable people who are retirement age and are retiring."
—*George W. Bush, Alexandria, Virginia, February 12, 2003*

A WHOLE LOTT OF TROUBLE

"**W**hen Strom Thurman ran for President we voted for him. We're proud of him. And if the rest of the country had followed our lead, we wouldn't have had all these problems over all these years either."

> —*Trent Lott, at a 100th birthday party for retiring South Carolina Senator Strom Thurmond, December 5, 2002*

What was probably meant as a compliment complicated Trent Lott's life tremendously and quickly ended his political career. You see, in 1948 Strom Thurmond ran for president as the State's Rights Democratic Party (Dixiecrats) candidate, and the main agenda of his campaign was supporting the continuing policies of segregation. So Trent was suggesting that segregation would have solved all our problems. His party turned on him faster than a pack of wild dogs, or wild elephants, if you will, and within weeks, Trent Lott had resigned from his position as Senate Majority Leader.

———————◆———————

"There is no such thing necessarily in a dictatorial regime of iron-clad absolutely solid evidence. The evidence I had was the best possible evidence that he had a weapon."

> —*George W. Bush,* Meet the Press, *February 8, 2004*

FLUFFY RICE

"**S**he's doing a fine job of coordinating interagency. She's doing what her—I mean—it shouldn'a—the, the, the role of the National Security Adviser is to not only provide good advice to the President, which she does on a regular basis—I value her judgment and her intelligence—uhh—but, uhh—her job is also to deal interagency, and to help unstick things that may get stuck—is the best way to put it. She's an unsticker. And—is she listening? Okay, well, she's doing a fine job."

—*George W. Bush, on National Security Adviser (now Secretary of State) Condoleezza Rice, Washington, D.C., October 28, 2003*

IN THE FISCAL YEAR 2002 FEDERAL BUDGET: $260,000 TO EXPLORE ASPARAGUS TECHNOLOGY.

WART ARE YOU LOOKING AT?

Duct tape has a new use—well, actually, U.S. Army researchers have found a new one: Use duct tape to remove those pesky warts. In 2002, Army researchers revealed that by covering a wart with duct tape, one can actually suffocate the growth and the resulting dead tissue can be easily removed with an emery board. Now you have a choice: Walk around with a wart or walk around with a wart covered with a piece of eye-catching tape.

"Security is the essential roadblock
to achieving the road map to peace."
—*George W. Bush, Washington, D.C., July 25, 2003*

OH, BROTHER!

In a deposition taken on March 4, 2003, as part of the divorce proceedings between Neil Bush (President Bush's younger brother) and his wife Sharon Bush, Neil admitted to some shady practices in the boardroom and the bedroom. Marshall Davis Brown, lawyer for Sharon Bush, was baffled as to why Grace Semiconductor Manufacturing Corp., a firm backed by Jiang Mianheng, the son of former Chinese President Jiang Zemin, would pay Neil $2 million in stock over five years.

MARSHALL DAVIS BROWN: You have absolutely no educational background in semiconductors do you?

NEIL BUSH: That's correct.

MARSHALL DAVIS BROWN: And you have absolutely over the last ten, fifteen, twenty years not a lot of demonstrable business experience that would bring about a company investing $2 million in you?

NEIL BUSH: I personally would object to the assumption that they're investing $2 million in me.

In addition to receiving a contract worth $2 million for a job he's certainly not qualified for, Neil admitted that during various business trips to Asia he had had sex with several woman—but here's where the Bush magic comes in—they all approached him (some even so bold as to knock on his hotel door and ask for sex).

MARSHALL DAVIS BROWN: Mr. Bush, you have to admit it's a pretty remarkable thing for a man just to go to a hotel room door and open it and have a woman standing there and have sex with her.
NEIL BUSH: It was very unusual.

Ah, it's good to be the king. Or at least, the brother of the king.

"And I call upon the Iraqi people to reject violence, band together to insist that the country move toward a peaceful tomorrow. Iraq is changing for the better. I mean, look at the soccer team."
—*George W. Bush, Washington, D.C., May 20, 2004*

TERRORIST PLOT SUBPLOT

Best-selling author Tom Clancy wrote two books about a pilot flying a fuel-laden jet into the Capitol building killing the President and other leaders (*Debt of Honor,* 1994; *Executive Orders,* 1996). After the attacks of 9/11, U.S. Army officials wanted to find out what else terrorists might do, so they convened some Hollywood writers. Tom Clancy was not included at the October 2001 meeting, but in attendance were the writers of *Die Hard* and *Delta Force One,* which makes sense, but also invited were the writers of *Grease* and the TV show *MacGyver.* So be on the lookout for a six foot seven, bearded man on dialysis singing, "I'm the one that you want . . . oh, oh, oh, honey, the one that you want."

"I couldn't imagine somebody like Osama bin Laden understanding the joy of Hanukkah."
—*George W. Bush, Washington, D.C., December 10, 2001*

NOW WHAT WOULD MRS. MANNERS SAY?

"The principles I laid out in the course of the campaign, and the principles we laid out at the recent economic summit are still the principles I believe in. And that is nothing will change for those near our Social Security, payroll—I believe you were the one who asked me about the payroll tax, if I'm not mistaken—will not go up. And I know there's a big definition about what that means. Well, again, I will repeat. Don't bother to ask me. Or you can ask me. I shouldn't—I can't tell you what to ask. It's not the holiday spirit. It is all part of trying to get me to set the parameters apart from the Congress, which is not a good way to get substantive reform done."

—*George W. Bush, Washington, D.C., December 20, 2004*

THROUGH BUREAUCRATIC ERROR, SENSITIVE U.S. AIR FORCE SPY-PLANE PARTS, ORIGINALLY INTENDED FOR DESTRUCTION, WOUND UP IN PRIVATE HANDS IN JUNE 2002 AND WERE UP FOR AUCTION ON EBAY.

DON'T KNOW MUCH ABOUT GEOGRAPHY ...

In June 2001, students at Oakhill College in Lancashire, north-west England, were delighted to get a signed letter from President Bush in response to their written congratulations on his inauguration. The mesmerized class suddenly broke out into peals of laughter at this line in the letter: "As young Americans, you have an important responsibility, which is to become good citizens." The British students, after they wiped tears of laughter from their eyes, agreed that although Bush was the most powerful man in the world they could teach him a little about geography.

IN THE FISCAL YEAR 2004 FEDERAL BUDGET: $1.5 MILLION FOR A DEMONSTRATION PROJECT TO TRANSPORT NATURALLY CHILLED WATER FROM LAKE ONTARIO TO LAKE ONONDAGA.

GENDER BENDER

During a speech commemorating International Women's Week, President Bush took the podium and exclaimed:
"Earlier today, the Libyan government released Fathi Jahmi. She's a local government official who was imprisoned in 2002 for advocating free speech and democracy."
—*Washington, D.C., March 12, 2004*

Nothing wrong with this statement except for the small fact that Fathi Jahmi is a man, not a woman, and was therefore a poor choice for International Women's Week.

"I hope the Congress will extend the unemployment benefits for—for the American workers who don't have a job—soon, as quickly as possible."
—*George W. Bush, Washington, D.C., January 6, 2003*

HEY, IF YOU CAN GET UNEMPLOYMENT BENEFITS AND STILL HAVE A JOB, SIGN ME UP.

LET'S MAKE THIS BRIEF

During the June 10, 2002, White House press briefing, Press Secretary Ari Fleischer was asked a question about a claim the president had made. The reporter said, "[The President said] he read the report. I believe the report is 260-some pages—he meant he read the full report?" Fleischer responded, "Whenever presidents say they read it, you can read that to be he was briefed." Fleischer then halfheartedly joked that his honesty would cost him his job. Because you know, honesty is an attribute not favored by most politicians.

"[The Estate Tax is] on its way to being put to extinction. I say, on its way——you'll hear me talk in a minute that these——some of these taxes don't really go away. It's like they go away for a period of time, but they come back."

—*George W. Bush, Louisville, Kentucky, February 26, 2004*

IT'S ALWAYS FUN TO HEAR BUSH TRY TO EXPLAIN HOW THE ESTATE TAX REFORM OF 2001 WILL EXPIRE IN 2011.

WHAT'S ANOTHER NAME FOR THESAURUS?

BUSH: Maybe I should be a little less direct and be a little more nuanced, and say we support regime change.

REPORTER: That's a change though, isn't it—a change in policy?

BUSH: No, it's really not. Regime change was the policy of my predecessor, as well.

REPORTER: And your father?

BUSH: You know, I can't remember that far back. It's certainly the policy of my administration. I think regime change sounds a lot more civil, doesn't it? The world would be better off without him. Let me put it that way, though. And so will the future.

—*Press Conference with Tony Blair, Crawford, Texas, April 6, 2002*

"Uhh—I hear there's rumors on the, uhh, Internets that we're gonna have a—draft. We're not going to have a draft. Period."
—*George W. Bush, Second Presidential Debate, St. Louis, Missouri, October 8, 2004*

MAYBE THAT'S WHY MY CONNECTION IS SO SLOW—I'M HOOKED UP TO THE WRONG INTERNET.

HOGS HATE PORK—EVEN GROUNDHOGS

Punxsutawney Phil is known around the world for his ability to forecast the weather and for his starring role in *Groundhog Day*. But in December 2004, Phil had a walk-on role, in a photo op with Representative John Peterson (R-Pennsylvania). Peterson woke the groundhog from his winter slumber so he could promote the spending of $100,000 in taxpayer money for the Punxsutawney Weather Discovery Center. Either in reaction to his rude awakening, or the fact that not even a groundhog can stand to see so much money wasted, Phil urinated on the press conference table. If Punxsutawney Phil sees his shadow, it means six more weeks of winter. If he does not see his shadow, it means spring is just around the corner. But if he sees Congress wasting taxpayer money on pork-barrel projects—it means there's going to be a mess to mop up.

> "As a result of hardening the homeland against a bioterrorist attack with first-time responders, our neighborhoods will be ultimately safer for crime."
>
> —*George W. Bush, Denver, Colorado, February 8, 2002*

THE PHRASE IS FIRST-RESPONDERS, BUT BUSH FRE-QUENTLY CALLS THEM FIRST-TIME RESPONDERS AS IF THEY'RE NOVICES. ALSO, IT SOUNDS LIKE HE'S CLEARING THE PATH FOR WHOLESALE CIVIL UNREST BY MAKING OUR NEIGHBORHOODS "ULTIMATELY SAFER FOR CRIME."

BUILD THE FRAME FROM THE GROUND UP

"There's a lot of people in the Middle East who are desirous to get into the Mitchell process. And—but first things first. The—these terrorist acts and, you know, the responses have got to end in order for us to get the framework—the groundwork—not frame-work, the groundwork to discuss a framework for peace, to lay the—all right."

> —*George W. Bush, Crawford, Texas, August 13, 2001*

Bush is referring to, or trying to refer to, former Senator George Mitchell's report on Middle East peace.

IN THE FISCAL YEAR 2003 FEDERAL BUDGET: SENATE INTERIOR APPROPRIATIONS SUBCOMMITTEE RANKING MEMBER CONRAD BURNS (R-MONTANA) INCLUDED $1 MILLION FOR A DNA STUDY OF BEARS IN HIS HOME STATE.

MAY I HAVE THE ENVELOPE, PLEASE

The U.S. Department of the Interior declared the Fresno (California) Sanitary Landfill a historic landmark in addition to placing it on the National Register of Historic Places, lauding its pioneering methods of disposal. The landfill, the oldest in the nation, was opened in 1937 and closed in 1987, and its disposal methods were adopted by all builders of modern sanitary landfills. Hours after the announcement, however, the site was removed from the nomination list because numerous environmentalist groups complained. It seems the landfill already held a place of honor— a long-standing spot on the EPA's Superfund list of the worst polluted land in America.

"But as we insist that Congress be wise with your money, we're going to make sure we spend enough to win this war. And by spending enough to win a war, we may not have a war at all."

—*George W. Bush, Kennesaw, Georgia, February 20, 2003*

WHAT'S THE HURRY?

As of May 2003, 90 percent of gun purchasers went through instant criminal background checks on an FBI database. As of that date, the State Department's list of known foreign terrorists had not been entered into the database. Seems like Big Brother keeps looking in the wrong places.

BUSH: Andrew Biggs is with us. He is the Associate Commissioner for Retirement Policy of the Social Security Administration, Washington, D.C. In other words, he is an expert on the subject. Andrew, step forth. Let the people of Arkansas—no, sit forth—let the people of Arkansas—

DR. BIGGS: Thanks very much.

BUSH: Tell them whether or not we got a problem or not, from your perspective.

DR. BIGGS: Put simply, we do, in fact, have a problem.

BUSH: By the way, this guy—Ph.D. See, I was a C student. He's a Ph.D., so he's probably got a little more credibility. I do think it's interesting and should be heartening for all C students out there, notice who's the President and who's the adviser. All right, Andrew, get going. Andrew's got a good sense of humor.

—*Little Rock, Arkansas, February 4, 2005*

I SMELL A RAT

There are few consistencies between the Clinton and Bush administrations, but sticking it to Native-Americans is one of them. Federal judge Royce Lamberth criticized both administrations for what he called the government's squandering of more than $10 billion in Indian trust funds (payments for grazing, mining, logging, and oil-drilling on Indian land). The Department of the Interior has been required to manage the trust since 1887, but their record keeping leaves much to be desired. In 1999, the DOI complained that it was unable to examine some trust fund records because they had been filed in dilapidated rooms and were now so covered with rat feces they were hazardous. In October 2001, a status report was prepared for Judge Lamberth, but a number of department officials refused to sign the document because they didn't believe all the information was truthful.

I can hear it now: "Is that a comma there? Ah, gross!"

"We can compete with anybody—at least, I think so."
—*George W. Bush, Washington, D.C., March 16, 2004*

BUT HOW DO YOU REALLY FEEL?

"**I** expressed myself rather forcefully, felt better after I had done it. I think that a lot of my colleagues felt that what I had said badly needed to be said—that it was long overdue." What was the Vice President of the United States referring to? A little intellectual banter on the Senate floor with Senator Patrick Leahy (D-Vermont) in which the VP told the senator to "F#*@ off!"

—June 22, 2004

"Congresswoman Melissa Hart, thank you for being here. ... Melissa happens to be a board of this community college system."
—George W. Bush, Pittsburgh, Pennsylvania, March 7, 2005

THREE STRIKES AND YOU'RE OUT

On April 14, 2005, a law adding lighters to the list of items not allowed on airplanes went into effect. The origin of the ban was the case of Richard Reid, who tried unsuccessfully to light explosives hidden in his shoes on a transatlantic flight in 2001, but he didn't use a lighter, he used matches. However, the newly enacted ban does not include matches, just lighters. Passengers may still bring aboard a plane up to four books of safety matches. The theory behind the new law is that if Reid had used a lighter he might have detonated the explosives. My theory is that if he wasn't a six-foot-four, shaggy-looking nutcase who attracted attention to himself by taking his sneakers off, he wouldn't even have needed a match. He could have rubbed two sticks together and have gotten away with it.

"We're still being challenged in Iraq and the reason why is a free Iraq will be a major defeat in the cause of freedom."
—*George W. Bush, Charlotte, North Carolina, April 5, 2004*

MY TRAIN OF THOUGHT
HAS DERAILED

"**I** bring up—I bring up a preacher because I want to thank all the preachers who are here, the pastors, those who shepherd. One pastor who is not here is my friend Jack Graham from Prestonwood Baptist. I bring that up because social entrepreneurs find out ways to leverage resources in a proper way. And what Tony Evans has done with Pastor Jack Graham, is to start an urban suburban and partnership."

—*George W. Bush, Dallas, Texas, October 29, 2003*

"We phased out the death tax, so America's family farmers can stay in the family."
—*George W. Bush, Davenport, Iowa, August 5, 2004*

OH, I THOUGHT YOU SAID "BOATING" RIGHTS

In January 2005, President Bush sat down with the Congressional Black Caucus for the first time in nearly four years. But what made the meeting more memorable was Bush's admission that he was "unfamiliar" with the Voting Rights Act of 1965. The Voting Rights Act is "generally considered the most successful piece of civil rights legislation ever adopted by the United States Congress," according to the description on the Department of Justice's Web site. Jesse Jackson, Jr., was so taken aback at the President's lack of knowledge on such a landmark piece of legislation that he quickly conferenced Congresswomen Maxene Waters (D-California), Sheila Jackson Lee (D-Texas) and his top legislative aide, to confirm "what he just said is what I heard." They all said he heard the President correctly.

Yup, as clear as black and white.

"Conservation may be a sign of personal virtue, but it is not a sufficient basis for a sound, comprehensive energy policy."
—*Vice President Dick Cheney, Toronto, Canada, May 1, 2001*

YOU LOOK MAAVELOUS

"**I** always jest to people, the Oval Office is the kind of place where people stand outside, they're getting ready to come in and tell me what for, and they walk in and get overwhelmed by the atmosphere. And they say, 'Man . . . you're looking pretty.'"
—*George W. Bush, Washington, D.C., November 4, 2004*

"Two and a half years ago—or two years ago, this nation came under enemy attack."
—*George W. Bush, Fort Stewart, Georgia, September 12, 2003*

THE INS ARE OUT

On March 1, 2003, the Immigration and Naturalization Service (INS) was incorporated into the newly formed Department of Homeland Security and just in time, too. An investigation in November 2002 revealed that the INS had granted citizenship to a man with ties to the radical Islamic group Hezbollah during a time he was under direct scrutiny by a joint FBI-NYPD terrorist task force! But that's not all. A short one week later, a General Accounting Office (GAO) review uncovered that the INS was unable to locate nearly half of the 4,100 supposedly registered immigrants the federal government wanted to interview in the days following the attacks of September 11, 2001. Apparently the INS had been ineffective in enforcing its own registration laws.

"Our enemies are innovative and resourceful, and so are we. They never stop thinking about new ways to harm our country and our people, and neither do we."
—*George W. Bush, Washington, D.C., August 4, 2004*

I'LL TAKE TRIBAL SOVEREIGNTY
FOR 400, ALEX

A reporter for the *Seattle Post-Intelligencer,* Mark Trahant, who is a member of Idaho's Shoshone-Bannock Tribe and former president of the Native American Journalists Association, accidentally stumped and confused President Bush at the 2004 conference of UNITY: Journalists of Color, Inc.:

TRAHANT: What do you think tribal sovereignty means in the twenty-first century, and how do we resolve conflicts between tribes and the federal and state governments?

BUSH: Yeah—tribal sovereignty means that, it's sovereign. It's— you're a—you're a—you've been given sovereignty, and you're—viewed as a sovereign entity. [Laughter ripples through the audience]

TRAHANT: Okay.

BUSH: And, therefore, the relationship between the federal government and tribes is one between—sovereign entities.

—*Washington, D.C., August 6, 2004*

"... we look forward to analyzing and working with legislation that will make—it would hope—put a free press's mind at ease that you're not being denied information you *shouldn't* see."
—*George W. Bush, Editors' Convention, April 14, 2005*

ALL SUBSTANCE, NO STYLE

The phrase "The Ugly American" still holds true today, particularly because of the actions of our President and Vice President. In January 2005, Vice President Dick Cheney attended a solemn ceremony in Poland remembering the sixtieth anniversary of the liberation of Auschwitz. Surrounded by a sea of black-coated somber dignitaries, the Vice President wore a fur-lined hooded olive drab ski parka (with his name embroidered on the pocket), brown leather lace-up boots, and a knit cap with the words "Staff 2001" embroidered on it. While all the other dignitaries, including French President Jacques Chirac and Russian President Vladimir Putin, wore dark, formal overcoats, dress shoes or boots, and either fedoras or fur hats, the Vice President "was dressed in the kind of attire one typically wears to operate a snow blower," wrote Robin Givhan, the *Washington Post*'s fashion writer.

Wait—I thought George W. Bush was accused of being a snow blower.

During a tour of Europe in May 2002 designed to elicit support for the U.S. war on terror, President Bush prepared to sign a historic nuclear arms reduction pact with Russia. With Russian President Vladimir Putin at his side, George Bush, who was chewing gum at the time, spit the gum into his hand, took up the pen, signed the document, and then stuck the gum back into his mouth.

At least he didn't stick it up under the desk.

Undersecretary of State John Bolton declared that whether Saddam actually possessed Weapons of Mass Destruction (WMDs), "isn't really the issue.... The issue, I think, has been the capability that Iraq sought to have... WMD programs."
—*United States Embassy, Paris, France, September 4, 2003*

DUBYA SPEAK—DOUBLESPEAK

REPORTER: Mr. President, why are you and the Vice President insisting on appearing together before the 9/11 Commission? And, Mr. President, who will you be handing the Iraqi government over to on June 30?

BUSH: We will find that out soon. That's what Mr. Brahimi [U.N. envoy Lakhdar Brahimi] is doing. He's figuring out the nature of the entity we'll be handing sovereignty over. And, secondly, because the 9/11 Commission wants to ask us questions, that's why we're meeting. And I look forward to meeting with them and answering their questions.

REPORTER: I was asking why you're appearing together, rather than separately, which was their request.

BUSH: Because it's a good chance for both of us to answer questions that the 9/11 Commission is looking forward to asking us, and I'm looking forward to answering them.

—*Prime Time Press Conference, Washington, D.C., April 13, 2004*

IN THE FISCAL YEAR 2004 FEDERAL BUDGET: $100,000 FOR THE UNIVERSITY OF PITTSBURGH CENTER FOR SPORTS MEDICINE TO DETERMINE THE PREVALENCE OF KNEE INJURIES IN FEMALE ATHLETES.

RED IN THE FACE AND ON THE NECK

According to the German news source *Der Spiegel,* in May 2002, a conversation between then Brazilian President Fernando Henrique Cardoso and President George Bush took a weird turn when Bush asked his colleague, "Do you have blacks, too?" Condoleezza Rice, then National Security adviser, jumped to her boss's aid by stating, "Mr. President, Brazil probably has more blacks than the U.S.A. Some say it's the country with the most blacks outside Africa." Later, President Cardoso commented that when it came to Bush's knowledge of Latin America he was still in his "learning phase." At least Bush's knowledge of Latin America stretched far enough that he didn't ask if they all spoke Latin.

[PRESIDENT] BUSH "DRAMATICALLY LESS VISIBLE"

—*AP headline, March 5, 2001*

THEN WE'RE OFF TO ROME, GEORGIA

REPORTER 1: You're not going to Athens this week, are you?
BUSH: Athens, Texas?
REPORTER 1: Ol—the Olympics, in Greece.
BUSH: Oh, the Olympics? No, I'm not.
REPORTER 2: Have you been watching them?
BUSH: Oh, yeah, yeah, it's been exciting.
REPORTER 2: Any particular moment stand out?
BUSH: Umm—particular moment? I like the—let's see—uhhhm—
Iraqi soccer. I liked—I liked seein' the Afghan woman
carryin' the flag comin' in. I loved, uhh—you know, our
gymnasts. I've been watching the swimming. I like th'—
I've seen a lot, yeah. Listen, thank you all.

—Crawford, Texas, August 23, 2004

"[Osama bin Laden is] either alive and well or alive and not too well or not alive."

*—Secretary of Defense Donald Rumsfeld, as quoted in
the* New Republic, *October 7, 2002*

DON'T TEE OFF THE PRESIDENT, PART ONE

It was a beautiful Sunday morning when President Bush rose early to enjoy a round of golf with his father at the Cape Arundel Golf Club in Kennebunkport, Maine. The President was approached by the media interested in a response about the recent suicide bombing in Israel. With golf club in hand, and waggling his finger to show resolve, Bush stated, "There are a few killers who want to stop the peace process that we have started. We must not let them." Pleased with not making any grammatical errors in his statement, the President thanked the reporters but before they could turn their cameras off, smiled and said, "Now watch this drive."

P.S. He hit the ball into the rough.

IN THE FISCAL YEAR 2005 FEDERAL BUDGET: $150,000 FOR EDUCATION PROGRAMS AT THE GRAMMY FOUNDATION IN SANTA MONICA.

NOTE: Revenues in 2003 for the U.S. motion picture and sound recording industries reached $78 billion.

"WITH ALL DUE

RESPECT

TO THE CAMERAS,

I HOPE YOU READ MORE

THAN YOU WATCH TV."

—*George W. Bush, Clarke Street Elementary School,*
Milwaukee, Wisconsin, May 8, 2002

THE INSULTED CAMERAS SNAPPED THEIR LENS
COVERS ON AND, STOMPING THE LEGS OF THEIR
TRIPODS, ANGRILY MARCHED OUT OF THE ROOM.

YOUR GOVERNMENT AT WORK

In a report issued in October 2003, the General Accounting Office (GAO) revealed that the Pentagon was less than diligent in keeping track of who was buying its surplus biological and chemical equipment. The GAO concluded that these items could easily have wound up in the hands of terrorists, obtained at substantial discounts. "Yes, I'd like to buy a bunch of surplus biological equipment, please. My name, sure, it's Ben Laden . . . no, B.E.N. Great. I'd like . . ."

"We spend money on research and development to expand the use of renewables, technologies to help us live different ways at the same lifestyle we're accustomed to."
—*George W. Bush, Colorado Springs, Colorado, October 12, 2004*

SOMEONE NEEDS TO GOVERN
THE PRESIDENT

"**O**ne of the most meaningful things that's happened to me since I've been the governor—the President—governor—President. Oops. Ex-governor. I went to Bethesda Naval Hospital to give a fellow a Purple Heart, and at the same moment I watched him— get a Purple Heart for action in Iraq—and at that same—right after I gave him the Purple Heart, he was sworn in as a citizen of the United States—a Mexican citizen, now a United States citizen."

—George W. Bush, January 9, 2004

"Pennsylvania's unemployment rate is 5.1 percent. That's good news for people who are trying to find jobs."
—George W. Bush, Smoketown, Pennsylvania, July 9, 2004

WATER YOU LOOKING AT?

During the Quebec City summit in April 2001, the new President sat down for dinner to dine on "Symphony Gaspesienne" and "Pommes de terre dauphinoise." All eyes were on the President as this was his first extended foreign excursion, and those eyes widened when they viewed Bush's table manners. At the well-appointed table in the ballroom, a chilled bottle of water and a crystal glass awaited the guests. Bush plopped down in his chair, grabbed the water bottle, twisted off the cap, and chugged it down. As Americans the only thing we're grateful for is that he didn't give out a Texas-sized belch.

"The *United States and the U.S.* stand together in support of the Iraqi people and the new Iraqi government, which will soon come into action."
—*George W. Bush, Brussels, Belgium, February 22, 2005*

THE MARCH HARE

"**T**he march to war affected the people's confidence. It's hard to make investment. See, if you're a small business owner or a large business owner and you're thinking about investing, you've got to be optimistic when you invest. Except when you're marching to war, it's not a very optimistic thought, is it? In other words, it's the opposite of optimistic when you're thinking you're going to war."
—*George W. Bush, Springfield, Missouri, February 9, 2004*

"This is fantastic! I've got a laser pointer! Holy mackerel!"
—*Secretary of Defense Donald Rumsfeld, DOD Press Briefing, November 27, 2001*

FOOD, IT'S WHAT'S FOR DINNER

The planners at the Pentagon had a color-scheme problem to contend with: what color should they use for the food packets they dropped over Afghanistan? They ruled out light blue because they thought the Afghanis would object, since it's the predominant color in the Israeli flag. They had been using a yellow wrap, but they were also dropping cluster bombs in yellow too. That forced them to actually drop fliers telling people that the square yellow packages were food and the cylindrical yellow packages were bombs: open the former and avoid the latter. Red was removed from the list because it could be misconstrued as packets of blood being dropped. How about a lovely shade of green? Nope, it might drop in a patch of dense grass and be overlooked—we know how much dense grass there is in the desert. How about purple? Sorry, purple is the color of royalty, and we don't want people thinking the food is meant for a king. My thought is, why bother with color? Do what the generic food distributors do—use a plain white wrapper with the word "FOOD" emblazoned in black. Or would that just be too tacky?

"I believe we are called to do the hard work to make our communities and quality of life a better place."

—*George W. Bush, Collinsville, Illinois, January 5, 2005*

A LITTLE TWO-STEP

REPORTER: The Bush Senior Administration and the Clinton Administration both had contingency plans in place for succession of the vice presidency. In part, that was because the Twenty-fifth Amendment is unclear about when a Vice President may be removed beyond the question of retirement, resignation, or death. Do you all have anything similar?

ARI FLEISCHER: I don't even think it's appropriate, in the context of what took place yesterday [Cheney's heart attack], to be discussing that topic from here.

REPORTER: Well, it certainly is appropriate. I mean, he had a health issue, and the whole reason that these contingency plans are in place is for something unexpected.

—*Press Briefing by then White House Press Secretary Ari Fleischer, March 7, 2001*

"For years, when we grew up— at least us baby boomers grew up— we thought that oceans would protect us from harm's way."

—*George W. Bush, Minneapolis, Minnesota, April 26, 2004*

GEOGRAPHY 101

During a high-level meeting in the Oval Office in December 2002, President Bush, along with ranking senators and members of the House, discussed the U.S.–sponsored "road map" for peace between the Israelis and Palestinians. Tom Lantos (D-California) suggested using the Swedish Army since the parties involved had positive views of Scandinavian countries. The President stared at the congressman inquisitively and said, "I don't know why you're talking about Sweden. They're the neutral one. They don't have an army." Trying to give the President a gracious way out of an embarrassing situation Lantos stated, "Mr. President, you may have thought that I said Switzerland. They're the ones that are historically neutral, without an army." But Bush wouldn't be swayed by something as silly as facts, "No, no, it's Sweden that has no army." The entire room fell silent until someone was kind enough to change the subject. A few weeks later, at the White House Christmas party, the President pulled Congressman Lantos aside and said, "You were right, Sweden does have an army."

ENERGY EXECUTIVES URGE
SOME GAS-EMISSION LIMITS ON BUSH
—New York Times *headline, August 1, 2001*

IT'S HARD TO BE HUMBLE
WHEN YOU'RE SO GREAT

"**O**ur country puts $1 billion a year up to help feed the hungry. And we're by far the most generous nation in the world when it comes to that, and I'm proud to report that. This isn't a contest of who's the most generous. I'm just telling you as an aside. We're generous. We shouldn't be bragging about it. But we are. We're very generous."

—*George W. Bush, Washington, D.C., July 16, 2003*

In the Fiscal Year 2004 Federal Budget:
$100,000 for the Alaska Sea Otter Commission.

I DIDN'T KNOW THERE WERE SO MANY SMART SEA OTTERS OUT THERE.

PIRACY ON THE HIGH SEAS

Here's a very specific request that was slid into the 2005 Omnibus Act, $2 million to the "Secretary of Navy for the purpose of acquiring a vessel with the Coast Guard registration number 225115." Sounds like a top-secret submarine, or some high-tech spy plane, but according to news sources, this is the USS *Sequoia,* the legendary presidential yacht. It has served more than nine Presidents, been meticulously restored, and was designated by Congress as a National Historic Landmark. In 1977, during President Jimmy Carter's Administration, the yacht was sold to demonstrate frugality and show that the President was tightening the government's belt. Now it looks like the yacht is going to the presidential dock again.

"I'm going to describe what we discussed a little earlier ...
We had a chance to visit with Teresa Nelson,
who's a parent, and a mom or a dad."
—*George W. Bush, Jacksonville, Florida, September 9, 2003*

MY STORY IS BIGGER THAN YOUR STORY

REPORTER: [The California recall is] the biggest political story in the country. Is it hard to go in there and say nothing about it?

BUSH: It is the biggest political story in the country? That's interesting. That says a lot. That speaks volumes.

REPORTER: You don't agree?

BUSH: It's up to—I don't get to decide the biggest political story. You decide the biggest political story. But I find it interesting that that is the biggest political story in the country, as you just said.

REPORTER: You don't think it should be?

BUSH: Oh, I think there's maybe other political stories. Isn't there, like, a presidential race coming up? Maybe that says something. It speaks volumes, if you know what I mean.

—Crawford, Texas, August 13, 2003

It might speak volumes but does anyone know what he means?

ON THE MORNING OF JUNE 29, 2002, VICE PRESIDENT DICK CHENEY BECAME THE SECOND MAN IN U.S. HISTORY TO BE ACTING PRESIDENT (WHILE PRESIDENT BUSH WAS UNDERGOING A COLONOSCOPY). THE FIRST MAN WAS VICE PRESIDENT GEORGE H. W. BUSH, WHO TOOK OVER THE RESPONSIBILITIES OF THE PRESIDENT WHILE RONALD REAGAN UNDERWENT SURGERY TO REMOVE CANCEROUS POLYPS FROM HIS COLON. DOES ANYONE SEE A THEME HERE?

ONE IN THE HAND
IS WORTH TWO IN THE BUSH

In December 2003, Vice President Cheney donned his camouflage suit, brought out his trusted shotgun, and went out with a couple of buddies on a hunting party. They loaded up their gear and trotted off to the Rolling Rock Club in Ligonier, Pennsylvania, to shoot pheasants that had been specially bred to be killed by the club's members and were released just for the Vice President's party. Cheney reportedly blasted 70 ringnecked pheasants plus some captive mallard ducks, and his party killed 417 of the approximately 500 pheasants released. A representative from the Humane Society lambasted the wholesale slaughter, stating that a clay-target shooting would be just as challenging: "This wasn't a hunting ground. It was an open-air abattoir." Just to show what a great sportsman he is, Cheney had all the birds plucked, quick-frozen, and sent to members of his staff. That's just like Cheney, giving people the bird.

"More Muslims have died at the hands of killers than— I say more Muslims—a lot of Muslims have died— I don't know the exact count—at Istanbul. Look at these different places around the world where there's been tremendous death and destruction because killers kill."

—*George W. Bush, Washington, D.C., January 29, 2004*

DON'T TEE OFF THE PRESIDENT, PART TWO

White House advisors pleaded with the president to "try not to look like you're on a golf course" after he made a statement regarding the assassination of an Afghan vice president. Before he got the somber news, Bush had played a game with his father at the Arundel Golf Club in Kennebunkport, Maine, and was preparing to celebrate his fifty-sixth birthday (July 6, 2002). He was in a playful mood and drew attention to his hat that had "El Jefe" written on it. "That's French," Bush boasted. Actually, it's Spanish for "the boss."

"It's in our country's interest to find those who would harm us and get them out of harm's way."

—*George W. Bush, Prime Time Press Conference,
Washington D.C., April 28, 2005*

I THOUGHT THESE WERE EXACTLY THE TYPE OF PEOPLE WE *DO* WANT IN HARM'S WAY.

THE UNWRITTEN RACE

"**A**nd then we'll be going to Gorée Island, where I'll be giving a speech about race, race in the world, race as it relates to Africa and America. And we're in the process of writing it. I can't give you any highlights of the speech yet because I, frankly, haven't seen it."

—*George W. Bush, Washington, D.C., July 3, 2003*

QUESTION: And finally, what are your plans after November?
SECRETARY DONALD RUMSFELD: I have . . .
QUESTION: I know you have more energy than everybody in this building combined.
SECRETARY DONALD RUMSFELD: I have not decided. That's something that—we'll jump off that bridge when we get to it.

—*Secretary of Defense Rumsfeld's interview with Rita Cosby, FOX, September 29, 2004*

NO, DUMBO IS THE ELEPHANT

During a trip to Botswana, to show America's concern for the
AIDS epidemic, President George W. Bush stopped by the
Mokolodi Nature Reserve for a photo op with African wildlife.
(The reserve is described as more of a zoo than a wildlife reserve.)
Bush's advance team positioned four elephants to give the most
dramatic effect possible, which meant not showing the President's
limo and the fence that surrounds the cheetahs. As Bush's yellow
truck rolled into frame, one of the elephants mounted another elephant in "a reproductive attempt." The President took the conju-
gal visit in stride, leaned over, and whispered something into Laura
Bush's ear—she responded by slapping him on the leg. Asked later
if the elephant, the symbol of the Republican Party, had strayed
off-message, Secretary of State Colin Powell remained as diplomatic
as ever. "The elephants were on message," he said, grinning. "We
were all on message."

BUSH VISITS BOTSWANA; HARD-HIT BY AIDS
—AP Headline, July 10, 2003

THANK YOU, MR. OBVIOUS

"**W**hatever amount of energy and effort is required from the White House, we will provide it, to get a bill done this summer, one that I can sign and then we can all go back to our districts—in my case, tour the country—and say we have accomplished a major objective. Together we work together."

—*George W. Bush, Washington, D.C., June 25, 2003*

And apart we work alone!

"I've got confidence in the Palestinians, when they understand fully what we're saying, that they'll make the right decisions. I can assure you, we won't be putting money into a society which is not transparent and corrupt, and I suspect other countries won't either."

—*George W. Bush, June 26, 2002*

GOING POSTAL

Representative Bob Schaffer of Fort Collins, Colorado, had wondered for years why post offices weren't named for ordinary people who face life's "extraordinary challenges." When given the chance to name a post office, Schaffer, a former member of a county mental health advisory board, immediately thought of Barney Apodaca, a man who is developmentally disabled, lives on his own, works two jobs, and raises money for charity. The bill H.R. 5308 passed unanimously and was signed into law by President Bush on November 6, 2002. There was only one problem: no one told Barney. "No one asked me if I wanted this. And if they did I would have said 'No!'" Barney said, when he found out later. "I don't want my name on the post office. I don't work over there. I never go to the post office," Barney wrote in a letter to Congressman Schaffer. "I feel like you are making fun of me and completely disrespecting my feelings." And if you're wondering what action Schaffer took to rectify the situation, you can write him at—301 South Howes Street in Fort Collins, Colorado, the Barney Apodaca Post Office.

"I have a record in office, as well. And all Americans have seen that record. September the fourth, 2001, I stood in the ruins of the Twin Towers. It's a day I will never forget."
—*George W. Bush, Marlton, New Jersey, October 18, 2004*

BACKWARD INTO THE FUTURE!

A GREASED POLL

"**T**here was a poll that showed me going up yesterday, not to be on the defensive. Actually I'm in pretty good shape politically, I really am. I didn't mean to sound defensive. But I am. Politicians, by the way, who pay attention to the polls are doomed, trying to chase opinion when what you need to do is lead, set the tone."
—*George W. Bush, Washington, D.C., October 14, 2003*

If politicians who pay attention to polls are doomed, and Bush was paying attention to a poll, what conclusion can one reach?

"These despicable [suicide attacks] were committed by killers whose only faith is hate. And the United States will find the killers, and they will learn the meaning of American justice."
—*George W. Bush, May 13, 2003*

BUT IF THE KILLERS DIED DURING THE SUICIDE ATTACK HOW CAN THEY BE BROUGHT TO JUSTICE?

MAY I HAVE THE ENVELOPE, PLEASE

Robert H. Kirkpatrick was surprised and delighted when he opened the envelope addressed to himself and realized it was from the Vice President of the United States. Inside was an invitation "to join the President and Mrs. Bush for a private dinner here in Washington, D.C. . . . and also ask you to serve as a representative of St. Clairsville, Ohio . . . to recognize your steadfast support of President Bush." The letter was delivered to Kirkpatrick not by a postman but by a guard because, you see, Kirkpatrick is serving time for cocaine possession at the Belmont Correctional Institution in St. Clairsville. I'm not sure what kind of support he can give the President from his current position, because as a felon he cannot vote.

"I'm also not very analytical. You know I don't spend a lot of time thinking about myself, about why I do things."
—*George W. Bush, aboard* Air Force One, *June 4, 2003*

WHO'S YOUR DADDY?

"I'm a big believer in the First Amendment, but often I'm incredibly uneasy about lines we have to draw. No one takes pleasure in trying to decide whether this potty-mouth word or that potty-mouth word is a violation of the law."

>—*Federal Communications Commission (FCC)*
>*Chairman Michael K. Powell (son of former Secretary of State*
>*Colin Powell) on indecency fines at a July 2004 symposium*

Fines for indecent programming exceeded $7.7 million in 2004, a huge increase from the $48,000 imposed the year before Powell became chairman. Well, you've got to draw a line somewhere—it might as well be through the First Amendment.

"This notion that the United States is getting ready
to attack Iran is simply ridiculous.
And having said that, all options are on the table."

>—*George W. Bush, Brussels, Belgium, February 22, 2005*

WHAT'S IN A NAME?

Just in time for the 2005 tax season, auditors for the U.S. Treasury Department tested computer security at the Internal Revenue Service. In April, they placed one hundred calls to random IRS employees claiming that they were from the tax agency's computer help desk and asked if they would change their password to one offered by the caller. By changing their passwords the IRS employees would make it possible for identity thieves to hack the IRS systems and get private taxpayer information. "We were able to convince thirty-five managers and employees to provide us their username and change their password," auditors said. A little more than a third of all the employees would have inadvertently opened up the IRS computer system to any number of viruses, hacking, and identity theft. But this ratio pales in comparison to a similar test done in 2001; at that time seventy-one out of one hundred IRS agents fell for the ruse.

QUESTION: Mr. Secretary, several of your generals have been talking about—

SECRETARY RUMSFELD: "Our generals," not "my generals"—our generals.

QUESTION: Well, our generals, America's generals have been talking about—you're obviously optimistic about the trend lines in Iraq. They've been talking—

SECRETARY RUMSFELD: They have not. I haven't seen a single general who has said that "I am optimistic."

—DOD Press Briefing, March 29, 2005

TAKING A LEAK

"We'll get to the bottom of this and move on. But I want to tell you something—leaks of classified information are a bad thing. And we've had them—there's too much leaking in Washington. That's just the way it is. And we've had leaks out of the administrative branch, had leaks out of the legislative branch, and out of the executive branch and the legislative branch, and I've spoken out consistently against them and I want to know who the leakers are."
—*George W. Bush, Chicago, Illinois, September 30, 2003*

Apart from the chronic and hilarious use of the words leak, leakers, and leaking, Bush creates a fourth branch of government, the "administrative branch."

"The math has changed. The math has changed this way. Baby boomers like me are getting ready to retire, and there's a lot of us. I turn sixty-two in 2008— it's a convenient date for me to retire."
—*George W. Bush, Tucson, Arizona, March 21, 2005*

BUSH SAYS 2008 IS A CONVENIENT TIME TO RETIRE— UNFORTUNATELY, HIS TERM DOESN'T END UNTIL 2009!

WE HAVE IT ON THE HIGHEST AUTHORITY

Christian Broadcasting Network (CBN) reported in June 2003 that it was no coincidence that following the Bush Administration's support of a separate Palestinian state, America suffered "the worst month of tornadoes in American history" with 375 twisters in eight days, along with other meteorological disasters. CBN said that God is punishing the United States for supporting the biblically unthinkable division of Israel. How reporters at CBN got an exclusive interview with God we will probably never know.

"First, let me make it very clear,
poor people aren't necessarily killers.
Just because you happen to be not
rich doesn't mean you're willing to kill."
—*George W. Bush, Washington, D.C., May 19, 2003*

AND THE AWARD GOES TO ...

"**I**t's a commission not only to convince our fellow citizens to love one another just like we like to be loved. It's a commission also to devise practical ways to encourage others to serve. And one practical way is for the development of an award that Americans from all walks of life all around our country will be able to post boldly on their wall, that says, 'I served this great country by loving somebody.'"

—*George W. Bush, Washington, D.C., January 30, 2003*

If loving someone makes a citizen worthy of winning an award, I'm going into the medal-making business!

"Health savings accounts are new. Anything new in society, when it comes to health, requires a certain amount of education. Now, if you're a small business like Sharon is, I want you to listen to these accounts."

—*George W. Bush, Annandale, Virginia, August 9, 2004*

A REAL TURKEY

The now-famous photograph of President Bush presenting a succulent turkey to troops in Baghdad on Thanksgiving 2003 has turned out to be a fake. Not the photograph—but the turkey—and I mean the bird. The soldiers were served their meals from cafeteria steam trays, and at the end of the buffet line was a life-size model of a turkey (apparently so the soldiers would know what they're eating). When the President arrived, he instinctively picked up the fake fowl and posed with the troops as if he were going to do the carving honors. When reporters got wind of the pretend poultry they asked Scott McClellan, Bush's press secretary, to come clean. McClellan made a rare joke by shifting attention to the White House Christmas tree due to be unveiled later and said: "The tree today, as far as I know, is real."

"Dr. [Raja] Khuzai also was there to have
Thanksgiving dinner with our troops.
And it turned out to be me, as well."

—*George W. Bush, Washington, D.C., March 12, 2004*

I'D LIKE SOME WHITE MEAT, STUFFING, CRANBERRY
SAUCE, AND A LITTLE SIDE DISH OF BUSH.

IF WORDS COULD KILL

"**T**he will of the United States can be shaken by suiciders . . . And suiciders who are willing to drive up to a Red Cross center, a center of international help and aid and comfort, and just kill. . . . The strategy remains the same. The tactics to respond to more suiciders driving cars will alter on the ground."
— *George W. Bush, Washington, D.C., October 28, 2003*

Bush coins a new word, "suiciders," and immediately puts it to good use.

"A small business owner's outlook is improved when there's a new product available that says, gosh, I'm meeting the needs of my employees and also being able to better control costs."
— *George W. Bush, Washington, D.C., March 16, 2004*

NOTHING COOLER THAN A NEW PRODUCT THAT CAN SPEAK!

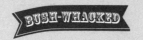
IN THE FISCAL YEAR 2005
FEDERAL BUDGET:

$1,540,000

FOR THE MISSOURI HISTORICAL
SOCIETY IN ST. LOUIS,
TO ESTABLISH AND MAINTAIN
AN ARCHIVE FOR MATERIALS
RELATING TO THE CONGRESSIONAL
CAREER OF THE HONORABLE
RICHARD A. GEPHARDT
(D-MISSOURI).

"WE'RE ON AN INTERNATIONAL MANHUNT FOR THOSE WHO WOULD DO HARM TO AMERICA, OR FOR ANYBODY ELSE WHO LOVES FREEDOM."

—*George W. Bush, Roswell, New Mexico, February 2, 2004*

BEWARE FREEDOM LOVERS, ACCORDING TO BUSH'S OWN WORDS, HE'S OUT TO GET YOU!

FORGET-ME-NOTS

During the vice presidential debate on October 5, 2004, Vice President Dick Cheney leveled John Edwards by saying, "Now, in my capacity as Vice President, I am the president of [the] Senate, the presiding officer. I'm up in the Senate most Tuesdays when they're in session. The first time I ever met you was when you walked on the stage tonight." That would be a devastating statement were it true, however:

• On February 1, 2001, Dick Cheney thanked John Edwards by name at a Senate prayer breakfast and sat beside him during the entire event.

• On April 8, 2001, Cheney and Edwards shook hands when they saw each other off-camera during a taping of NBC's *Meet the Press*.

• On January 8, 2003, the two met yet again when Edwards accompanied Elizabeth Dole to her swearing-in ceremony—conducted by Dick Cheney.

"I believe there's all kinds of brilliant and smart and
capable Palestinians that, given the chance,
given a chance to emerge—and by the way,
people committed to peace—and given the chance to
articulate that vision of peace will do so."

—*George W. Bush, Washington, D.C., July 31, 2002*

CAN YOU BE MORE DIRECT?

REPORTER: Are there linkages between al Qaeda and Iraq, and
where are they?

SECRETARY RUMSFELD: The deputy director of Central
Intelligence briefed me on that subject. I have no desire to
go beyond saying the answer is *yes*.

—*DOD Press Briefing, September 26, 2002*

THE REAL ENEMY—A RACK

It's hard to tell which one is the bigger boob, U.S. Attorney General John Ashcroft, or the bared breast on the statue the *Spirit of Justice.* The U.S. Justice Department (read: our tax money) spent $8,000 in January 2002 on curtains to hide the statue from the cameras. News photographers have had fun in the past snapping pictures with the breast strategically located next to Ashcroft's head. Ashcroft's decision sounds like a little tit-for-tat to me.

"It's amazing to me that we've got an enemy, on the one hand, that's willing to convince young males to commit suicide on behalf of a cause that's empty and, at the same time, try to escape the justice of America in caves."
—*George W. Bush, East Moline, Illinois, January 14, 2002*

SIZE DOES MATTER

"**I** think I've answered the question, and yes, [Arnold Schwarzenegger] would be a good governor, as would others running for governor of California. Like you, I'm most interested in seeing how the process evolves. It's a fascinating bit of political drama evolving in the state—in the country's largest state."
—*George W. Bush, Crawford, Texas, August 13, 2003*

Actually, Alaska is the country's largest state. But even giving him the benefit of the doubt that he was talking about the contiguous United States, California still isn't the largest state. As Bush should know, Texas, his home state, is larger than California.

"With the campaign over, Americans are expecting a bipartisan effort and results. I'll reach out to everyone who shares our goals."
—*George W. Bush, Washington, D.C., November 4, 2004*

ALTHOUGH THIS STARTS OFF SOUNDING LIKE AN ALL-INCLUSIVE STATEMENT IT ACTUALLY INCLUDES ONLY PEOPLE WHO AGREE WITH THE REPUBLICAN PARTY.

OFF TO A SLOW START

As we headed into August 2001 it came to the attention of the national media that President George Bush had spent less than two thirds of his days actually working. When the President announced he was going on a thirty-one-day vacation to Crawford, Texas, the press had a field day. The flak became so great that Bush's people convinced him to trim a week off so he wouldn't beat President Richard Nixon's record of thirty consecutive days off.

"It's hard to be successful if you don't make something somebody doesn't want to buy."

—*George W. Bush, Arlington, Virginia, March 9, 2004*

THAT MAKES SENSE, RIGHT?

"**W**e are in the process of helping them implement a strategy which is was described to us in Aqaba as to how the Palestinian Authority want to reconstitute a security force in order to make sure the terrorists, the haters of peace, those who can't stand free-dom do not have their way in the Middle East."

—*George W. Bush, Kennebunkport, Maine, June 15, 2003*

Maybe I didn't take all of my medication or I took all of my med-ication at once—but I'm confused.

"But the Congress giveth, the Congress taketh away.
And these tax relief will be—
will expire on an irregular basis."
—*George W. Bush, Washington, D.C., February 19, 2004*

SIGNED, SEALED, DELIVERED

An emergency room near Minneapolis, Minnesota, was vacated while postal inspectors and the Joint Terrorism Task Force of the FBI investigated a possible act of bioterrorism. A postal employee was admitted to the hospital in March 2003 complaining of a "headache and burning sensation" that he claimed was a direct result of handling a suspicious envelope. The white envelope was addressed to U.S. Rep. Dana Rohrabacher (R-California) and was lumpy and foul smelling. Upon opening the envelope authorities didn't discover Anthrax or a vial filled with the influenza virus; they did find a rotten potato slice and a note that read, "Have a French fry." Jim Ahlgren, a Postal Service spokesman said, "We assume it is a political statement having to do with the House [cafeteria] changing French Fries to Freedom Fries." As the note was nonthreatening and there are no laws barring the mailing of rotten food, officials will not take any action. However, authorities believe this to be the work of the Hamburglar: Mayor McCheese has been taken to an undisclosed location.

"I believe we ought to love our neighbor like we love ourself, as manifested in public policy through the faith-based initiative where we've unleashed the armies of compassion to help heal people who hurt."

—*George W. Bush, Third Presidential Debate, Tempe, Arizona, October 13, 2004*

THE 12 X 12 PRESIDENT

Responding to a reporter's question about how he envisions accomplishing U.S. goals in the Middle East, President George Bush got slightly off course. "See, one of the interesting things in the Oval Office—I love to bring people into the Oval Office—right around the corner from here—and say, this is where I office, but I want you to know the office is always bigger than the person."

—*Washington, D.C., January 29, 2004*

IN THE FISCAL YEAR 2002 FEDERAL BUDGET:
$50,000 FOR SAN LUIS OBISPO, CALIFORNIA,
TO REMOVE GANG MEMBERS' TATTOOS.

OKAY, THE HOW ABOUT THIS EXCUSE

During the vice presidential debate, Dick Cheney was asked about the justification for invading Iraq. Since no weapons of mass destruction had been found and the 9/11 Commission proved there was no connection between Saddam Hussein and Osama bin Laden (the two main arguments for the invasion), Cheney was in a bind for an explanation. Not skipping a beat he stated that Saddam's Iraq was harboring Abu Nidal, a Palestinian charged with masterminding acts of terrorism in the 1970s and 1980s, and that was the reason for the attack. The only problem with that logic was that Nidal had died in August 2002, two months before the Bush administration sought and was granted permission from Congress to engage in force against Iraq.

"And so, in my State of the—my State of the Union—or state—my speech to the—nation, whatever you wanna call it, speech to the nation—I asked Americans to give four thousand years—four thousand hours over the next— of the rest of your life—of service to America. That's what I asked. I said two—four thousand hours."

—*George W. Bush, Bridgeport, Connecticut, April 9, 2002*

· 87 ·

PERSON OF CONGRESS

"If you're a younger person, you ought to be asking members of Congress and the United States Senate and the President what you intend to do about it. If you see a train wreck coming, you ought to be saying, what are you going to do about it, Mr. Congressman, or Madam Congressman?"

—*George W. Bush, Detroit, Michigan, February 8, 2005*

"There is no doubt in my mind that this country cannot achieve any objective we put our mind to."

—*George W. Bush, Buffalo, New York, April 20, 2004*

WORKING HARD OR HARDLY WORKING?

In the first presidential debate with John Kerry, President Bush answered the first question from Jim Lehrer about another 9/11-type terrorist attack with, "No, I don't believe it's going to happen." And then he got tough with phrases like, "In Iraq, no doubt about it, it's tough. It's hard work. It's incredibly hard." He repeated the phrases "hard work," "working hard," "hard choices," "hardest" and other "hard"-based verbiage twenty-two times.

It's comforting to know our President is a hard-selling, hard-boiled, hardhanded, hardnosed, hard-ass, hardheaded, hard-baller who is hardly hard-up when hard-core hard-times are had.

"I just want you to know that, when we talk about war, we're really talking about peace."
—*George W. Bush, Washington, D.C., June 18, 2002*

SUPERCALLIFRAGILISTIC-EXPIALIDOCIOUS

"**W**e actually misnamed the war on terror. It ought to be the 'struggle against ideological extremists who do not believe in free societies who happen to use terror as a weapon to try to shake the conscience of the free world.'"

—George W. Bush, Washington, D.C., August 6, 2004

Uh, come to think of it, the "War on Terror" works for me.

IN THE FISCAL YEAR 2005 FEDERAL BUDGET: $300,000 FOR WOOL RESEARCH (MONTANA, TEXAS, AND WYOMING). THE MAIN PROBLEM WITH THIS PIECE OF PORK IS THAT WOOL PRICES ARE HEADING TOWARD LEVELS THEY HAVEN'T SEEN IN EIGHT TO TEN YEARS. SINCE 1984, $4.6 MILLION HAS BEEN APPROPRIATED FOR THIS RESEARCH.

BORED AT BOARDING

The Federal Aviation Administration admitted in February 2002 that passengers had to go back through security at Louisville International Airport because a security screener had fallen asleep. One American Airlines flight had to be brought back to the terminal and emptied. The newly formed Transportation Security Administration had only weeks before taken over security in airports. Approximately one thousand people passed through the screening process while the security screener snoozed. Because he's a security screener from the Transportation Security Administration, you can bet he's got job security, too.

"The Iraqi regime is a threat to any American and to threats who are friends of America."

—*George W. Bush, Fort Hood, Texas, January 3, 2003*

GUILTY UNTIL PROVEN GUILTY

"**S**addam Hussein had biological and chemical weapons that were unaccounted for that we're still confident we'll find. I think the burden is on those people who think he didn't have weapons of mass destruction to tell the world where they are . . . just because they haven't yet been found doesn't mean they didn't exist. The burden is on the critics to explain where the weapons of mass destruction are. If they think they were destroyed, the burden is on them to explain when he destroyed them and where he destroyed them."

> —*Press Briefing by then White House Press Secretary Ari Fleischer,*
> *Washington, D.C., July 9, 2003*

How he said that with a straight face is a mystery.

"And I'm glad Laura is here tonight. In my book,
she's a fabulous First Lady. And I love her a lot and I hope
she loves me a lot for dragging her out of Texas."

> —*George W. Bush, Dallas, Texas, July 18, 2003*

A DOSE OF SARCASM

Susan Sheybani, an assistant to Bush campaign manager Terry Holt, has the perfect prescription for American workers displeased with low-quality jobs. "Why don't they get new jobs if they're unhappy—or go on Prozac?" she was overheard saying to a colleague who was transferring a phone call from a reporter. Whoops, wrong time to make a remark like that. When it came to her attention in July 2004 that her comment was making all the newspapers, Sheybani said, "Oh, I was just kidding." This time she made the remark on the record.

"The [military] academies are really important for a lot of reasons. Obviously, what you learn on the football field is even more important since we're still at war."
—*George W. Bush, Washington, D.C., May 16, 2003*

NORTH BY NORTHWEST

REPORTER: You talk about the general threat toward Americans.
. . . And people ask us, what is it they're supposed to be on
the lookout for? What are Americans supposed to look for
and report to the police or to the FBI?

BUSH: You know, if you find a person that you've never seen before
getting in a crop-duster that doesn't belong to you, report
it . . ."

—Press Conference, October 11, 2001

AFTER THE UNITED STATES ACKNOWLEDGED
THAT A SPECIAL FORCES RAID ON HAZAR
QADAM, AN AFGHAN VILLAGE, ON JANUARY 24,
2002, LEFT EIGHTEEN AFGHANS WHO WEREN'T
MEMBERS OF THE TALIBAN OR AL QAEDA DEAD,
GENERAL TOMMY FRANKS SAID HE WOULD "NOT
CHARACTERIZE IT AS A FAILURE OF ANY TYPE."

SHOT IN THE FOOT

One of the reasons President Bush thought it necessary to create the Department of Homeland Security was that there was little or no communication between existing departments such as the Justice Department and the FBI. In fact, less than two months after the attacks of 9/11, the Justice Department refused to let the FBI check their records involving gun buyers to see if any of the 1,200 people detained after September 11 had purchased weapons. This rule is in keeping with Attorney General John Ashcroft's strong support of gun rights and his opposition to using the National Instant Criminal Background Check System to check records. The Bureau of Alcohol, Tobacco and Firearms keeps a database of guns used in the commission of a crime, and it found thirty-four guns had been bought at some point by people on the detainee list.

"I think that we believe there are
chemical weapons in Syria."
—*George W. Bush, Washington, D.C., April 13, 2003*

YOU'RE DOING FINE, OKLAHOMA!
OKLAHOMA—O.K.

During an interview with Ron Insana of CNBC on the tenth anniversary of the Oklahoma City bombing, President Bush was asked to discuss his feelings on the bombing and its relationship to the war on terror.

PRESIDENT BUSH: It goes to show that violence can erupt anywhere, any time, and, and as a society we've got to be diligent to those who would try to harm us. It also goes to show that terrorist acts not only come from abroad but can come here at home. The positive news in this instance is the City of Oklahoma came together in strong compassion and decency and care and hope for those who suffered, and our justice system worked.

>   —*Interview with Ron Insana of CNBC, April 19, 2005*

"Excuse me, I'm trying to get to the City of Oklahoma but I can't seem to find it on my map."

"I was a prisoner too, but for bad reasons."
—*George W. Bush, remarking to Argentine President Nestor Kirchner, after being told that all but one of the Argentine delegates to a summit meeting were imprisoned during the military dictatorship, Monterrey, Mexico, January 13, 2004*

TWO IN THE BUSH

In late February 2001, at his first meeting with a European leader, President George W. Bush brought British Prime Minister Tony Blair to Camp David. Newly fallen snow covered the ground at the secluded presidential retreat in Maryland's Catoctin Mountains, while Bush and Blair stood in front of a glowing fire addressing a group of reporters. When one of them asked the leaders to name some things they have in common, Bush chimed in, "We both use Colgate toothpaste." Blair, taken aback by the outing, replied, "They're going to wonder how you knew that, George." Remember, don't ask, don't tell.

This isn't the only time Bush made such a queer comment. Later in that same year, November 13, 2001, while meeting with Russian President Vladimir Putin, Bush said, "You're the kind of guy I like to have in a foxhole with me."

IN THE FISCAL YEAR 2005 FEDERAL BUDGET: $80,000 FOR THE SAN DIEGO GAY, LESBIAN, BISEXUAL, AND TRANSGENDER COMMUNITY CENTER.

WINNING IS NOT AN OPTION

"**A**nd we'll be tough and resolute as we unite, to make sure freedom stands, to rout out evil, to say to our children and grandchildren, we were bold enough to act, without tiring, so that you can live in a great land and in a peaceful world. And there's no doubt in my mind, not one doubt in my mind, that we will fail."
—*George W. Bush, Washington, D.C., October 4, 2001*

A classic example of Bush either speaking the truth or making a mistake—a few weeks after the attacks of September 11, 2001.

Top Pentagon and CIA officials met with Michael Drosnin, the author of *The Bible Code,* who claimed Osama bin Laden's whereabouts could be detected by connecting letters from ancient Hebrew.
—Wall Street Journal, *February 28, 2002*

DICK LICKS THE DRAFT

During the bitter fighting between the two sets of candidates in the 2004 presidential election, Dick Cheney continually questioned John Kerry's service in Vietnam. Kerry enlisted in the Navy months before he graduated from Yale and wound up receiving three Purple Hearts, the Bronze Star, and the Navy's Silver Star for gallantry in action. Kerry won five medals— Cheney won *five* deferments. Here's the Cheney story during the Vietnam war years.

1963 (JANUARY): Vietnam is heating up. Cheney enrolls in Casper Community College and gets his first deferment as a college student.

1963 (JULY): Transfers to the University of Wyoming at Laramie and obtains his second student deferment.

1964 (OCTOBER): Cheney marries his high school sweetheart, Lynne, and is granted his third student deferment.

1965 (NOVEMBER): Cheney starts graduate school (University of Wyoming) and receives his fourth student deferment.

1965 (OCTOBER 6): Selective Service lifts the ban against drafting married men who have no children. Nine months and two days later, Cheney's first daughter, Elizabeth is born. Cheney applies for a 3-A "hardship" exemption, which excludes men with children or dependent parents. It is granted, giving him his fifth military deferment in three years.

·99·

In his Senate confirmation hearings as defense secretary in 1989 under the first President Bush, Cheney claimed he "would have obviously been happy to serve had I been called." However, when he was away from the hearing room, he told the *Washington Post* the real reason he sought so many deferments was "I had other priorities in the sixties than military service."

"Under the dictator, prisons like Abu Gar——reb—— were symbols of death and torture...
When that prison is completed, detainees at Abu Garomp will be relocated. Then, with the approval of the Iraqi government, we will demolish the Abu Garab prison, as a fitting symbol of Iraq's new beginning."
—*George W. Bush, Carlisle, Pennsylvania, May 24, 2004*

FACTS ARE STUPID THINGS

During a radio interview in Phoenix, Arizona, on August 26, 2004, Secretary of Defense Donald Rumsfeld granted an interview to *Real Life with David Leibowitz* on KTAR-AM 620. Rumsfeld was dead set against admitting that any abuses occurred during interrogations at the Abu Ghraib prison.

SECRETARY RUMSFELD: I think the interesting thing about the Schlesinger Panel is there is a conclusion that, in fact, the abuses seem not to have anything to do with interrogation at all and any suggestion to the contrary, it would seem to me, would be incorrect given what we know at the present time, as a result of their report. These were apparently acts of abuse that took place not in the context of interrogating people . . .

Actually, if you really scrubbed the document, say all the way down to the fifth sentence of the first paragraph, you would read: "[W]e do know that some of the egregious abuses at Abu Ghraib which were not photographed did occur during interrogation sessions and that abuses during interrogation sessions occurred elsewhere."

"Justice ought to be fair."
—*George W. Bush, Washington, D.C., December 15, 2004*

JANE, STOP THIS CRAZY THING!!
JAAAAAANNNNNNEEEEE!

Attempting to show off his understanding of modern technology, President Bush, tennis racket in hand, jumped onto a Segway Human Transporter for a photo op. As cameras clicked away Bush stepped on the machine and immediately fell off. There was great speculation as to what could have happened and why the President couldn't stay balanced on this self-balancing machine. After studying all the possibilities, the makers of the Segway have figured it out—Mr. Bush had forgotten to turn the machine on.

GEORGE W. BUSH GAVE KARL ROVE, HIS ADVISER AND CAMPAIGN STRATEGIST, THE NICKNAME "TURD-BLOSSOM."

"AND SO I'M GOING TO SPEND A LOT OF
TIME ON SOCIAL SECURITY.

I ENJOY IT.

I ENJOY TAKING ON THE ISSUE.
I GUESS, IT'S THE

MOTHER

IN ME."

—*George W. Bush, Editors' Convention, April 14, 2005*

E.T. PHONE HOME

There must be a problem with illegal aliens in this country, and I'm not talking about people without green cards. I'm talking about card-carrying little green men. Included in the 2005 Defense Budget is $1.5 million for the Allen Telescope Array at the University of California, Berkley. This telescope is part of the Search for Extraterrestrial Intelligence Institute (SETI) whose Web site mentions that funding for the telescope was given by Paul Allen (cofounder of Microsoft) and Nathan Myhrvold (former Chief Technology Officer for Microsoft), but fails to mention the huge grant given by you, the taxpayer. The Web site also doesn't mention how this telescope will be used for defense (seems like it would since the money came out of the Defense Budget) unless, of course, we're attacked by aliens.

"It's only fair if other countries treat us
the way they treat them."
—*George W. Bush, Columbus, Ohio, September 1, 2004*

TEXAS TAXES

"**T**he problem we have, and the reason we have to continue to talking about this issue is because of a quirk in the Senate rules. Let me just put it to you this way, in plain language. The Senate has got the kind of rule where you pass the tax cut and then ten years it goes back to where we were. The way I like to put it, if I can—in plain English is, on the one hand, they taketh away, on the other hand, they giveth. On the one hand they give tax relief, on the other hand, you don't get tax relief. It's hard to explain in Manchester, New Hampshire, and it's darn sure hard to explain in Crawford, Texas."
—*George W. Bush, Manchester, New Hampshire, October 5, 2002*

What he is trying to explain, while insulting the people of Crawford's intelligence, is the fact that the Estate Tax Reform of 2001 will expire in 2011. The legislation includes a provision that *automatically reinstates the tax* at the end of the ten-year period, unless Congress passes new legislation continuing the repeal.

"But, nevertheless, I think long term, the stock market is, will reflect the long-term strength of America."
—*George W. Bush, interview with Ron Insana of CNBC, April 19, 2005*

THIS IS TRUE. AND IN THE SHORT TERM, THE STOCK MARKET WILL REFLECT THE SHORT-TERM STRENGTH OF AMERICA. IN THE MID-TERM, THE STOCK MARKET WILL REFLECT THE MID-TERM STRENGTH OF AMERICA—AND SO ON.

HERE, THERE, AND EVERYWHERE

"The area . . . that coalition forces control . . . happens not to be the area where weapons of mass destruction were dispersed. We know where they are. They're in the area around Tikrit and Baghdad and east, west, south, and north somewhat."
—*Secretary of Defense Donald Rumsfeld,*
This Week with George Stephanopoulos, *March 30, 2003*

**IN THE FISCAL YEAR 2003 FEDERAL BUDGET:
$500,000 FOR CATFISH HEALTH
IN STONEVILLE, MISSISSIPPI.**

"THE FIRST PART OF YOUR

QUESTION

IS THAT—IS WHETHER OR NOT

THE WEAPONS OF

MASS DESTRUCTION

QUESTION."

—*George W. Bush, St. Petersburg, Russia, June 1, 2003*

HE'S JUST A BIG, LOVABLE TEDDY BEAR

"There's only one person who hugs the mothers and the widows, the wives, and the kids, upon the death of their loved one. Others hug but having committed the troops, I've got an additional responsibility to hug and that's me and I know what it's like."
—*George W. Bush, Washington, D.C., December 11, 2002*

So apparently in addition to the responsibilities of running the most powerful country in the free world, serving as Commander in Chief during a time of war, restructuring the government to ward off potential terrorist attacks, and pulling us out of a sluggish economy, his other duty is to hug people?

THE DEFENSE THREAT REDUCTION AGENCY CONFESSED IN SEPTEMBER 2003 THAT IT HAD BEEN ACTIVELY MONITORING, VIA THE INTERNET, A WEBCAM OF A FACILITY IN SCOTLAND'S ISLE OF ISLAY BECAUSE IT RESEMBLED A CHEMICAL FACTORY. UPON CLOSER SCRUTINY, IT TURNED OUT TO BE A WHISKEY DISTILLERY.

AND THE AWARD GOES TO . . .

The number of Bronze Stars for Meritorious Service (not Valor, which is a separate category) grew substantially in the post 9/11 conflicts (Afghanistan, Iraq, Philippines). Here are some examples of service members who were awarded this coveted medal:

• An Army captain who merely supervised the distribution of 3,500 maps to his troops.

• Five submarine commanders whose sailors simply did the job they were supposed to do and fired cruise missiles at Iraqi targets.

• A sergeant who accidentally electrocuted himself.

• Another sergeant who was hit by friendly fire when the soldier behind him tripped and accidentally shot him in the back.

I understand that giving out awards boosts morale, but if you start giving out too many medals, it tarnishes the honor.

"The definition of a patriot in the face of the evil done to America is to serve something greater than yourself in life, is to help somebody in need, is to love a person one at a time, as we remember that—which I know we will."

—*George W. Bush, Manchester, New Hampshire,*
October 5, 2002

THE DUBYA AND WEBSTER'S DICTIONARY

"If Russia thought that the neighborhood was unsettled, it might create some issues. But Poland has provided a great source of stability in the neighborhood, and therefore Russia feels less threatened. And I think that's an important nuance, as we say in foreign policy. I think that's the word, isn't it? Nuance?"

—*George W. Bush, Press Conference with President Aleksander Kwasniewski of Poland and his wife Jolanta Kwasniewska, Washington, D.C., July 17, 2002*

What I love about this quote is that he's not sure he's using the right word, and he isn't, and he begins the statement with "as we say in foreign policy."

"If he declares he has none [weapons of mass destruction], then we will know that Saddam Hussein is once again misleading the world."

—*Press Briefing by then White House Press Secretary Ari Fleischer, Washington, D.C., December 2, 2002*

BASICALLY, HE'S SADDAMED IF HE DOES AND HE'S SADDAMED IF HE DOESN'T.

BONUS? HE SURE DID

In December 2002, Marion "Spike" Bowman received a presidential citation and a large cash bonus (20 to 30 percent of his annual salary) for his work as head of the FBI's National Security Law Unit. Way to go, Spike! Once the distinction came to the attention of Congress, however, things started to unravel. Apparently his department was responsible for impeding the Minneapolis FBI office's pre-September 11 investigation of Zacarias Moussaoui. But not just that, a Senate investigation also criticized Spike's unit for blocking an urgent request on August 29, 2001, by FBI agents in New York to begin searching for Khalid Almihdar, who became one of the hijackers on the flight that crashed into the Pentagon. Senator Richard Shelby, of Alabama, the senior Republican on the Intelligence Committee, who headed an oversight investigation of the FBI, complained days before the award, fittingly called the Presidential Rank Award, that Spike's law unit gave "inexcusably confused and inaccurate information" to FBI investigators during the Moussaoui case that led agents on a "wild goose chase for nearly three weeks." Shelby said, "They continue to reward bad behavior, and the results speak for themselves."

"He [Osama bin Laden] is—as I mentioned in my speech, I do mention the fact that this is a fellow who is willing to commit youngsters to their death and he, himself, tries to hide—if, in fact, he's hiding at all."

—*George W. Bush, Washington, D.C., March 13, 2002*

GET BACK, HONKY CAT

REPORTER: The NAACP is meeting this week in Houston, as you probably know. And there's been some criticism that you've not attended their convention since the 2000 campaign. How would you respond to that, and respond generally to suggestions from some critics that your civil rights record in the administration is not a stellar one?

BUSH: Let's see. There I was, sitting around the leader with— the table with foreign leaders, looking at Colin Powell and Condi Rice.

—*George W. Bush, Washington, D.C., July 9, 2002*

Bush forgets to finish his sentence, or didn't actually have a sentence in mind, and just wanted to brag about the fact that he has two African-Americans in his administration. This is the political equal of, "Hey, some of my best friends are black."

SEVERAL MONTHS AFTER THE ATTACKS OF
SEPTEMBER 11, 2001, THE FBI CONTACTED
SOME PSYCHICS WHO HAD PREVIOUSLY
WORKED AS "REMOTE VIEWERS" WITH
U.S. INTELLIGENCE. "REMOTE VIEWERS"
ARE EXACTLY WHAT YOU THINK THEY ARE,
PEOPLE WHO CAN SEE INTO THE FUTURE.
THE FEDERAL GOVERNMENT HAD A
REMOTE-VIEWING PROGRAM THAT WAS
RUN FOR YEARS BY CALIFORNIA'S
STANFORD RESEARCH INSTITUTE, UNTIL
IT WAS SHUT DOWN IN 1995. I WONDER IF
THOSE PSYCHICS SAW IT COMING?

HOW DID SHE GET UP THERE?

While ABC's Peter Jennings was soberly delivering the news at 6:30 P.M. on April 22, 2003, the closed captioning of his words rolled by. A slip of the typist's fingers translated Peter's words that Federal Reserve Chairman Alan Greenspan was "in the hospital for an enlarged prostate" into "in the hospital for an enlarged prostitute." The following day, Greenspan's wife, Andrea Mitchell, announced that her husband was recuperating after prostate surgery and as for the "enlarged prostitute" Mitchell said, "He should be so lucky."

"There are a couple of cows waiting for me. You know, when I first got back from Washington, it seemed like the cows were talking back. But now that I've spent some time in Crawford, they're just cows."
—*George W. Bush, Ontario, California, January 5, 2002*

OKAY, DOES THIS PARAGRAPH SCARE THE HELL OUT OF ANYONE ELSE BUT ME?

NOW THAT'S A REAL SHAME

"There's an old . . . saying in Tennessee . . . I know it's in Texas, probably in Tennessee that says Fool me once . . . [three-second pause] . . . Shame on . . . [four-second pause] . . . Shame on you. . . . [six-second pause] . . . Fool me . . . Can't get fooled again."

—*George W. Bush, Nashville, Tennessee, September 17, 2002*

The phrase he was groping for is, "Fool me once, shame on you. Fool me twice, shame on me." I wonder if there's a phrase about letting someone fool you dozens of times?

When questioned about the still unfound Weapons of Mass Destruction, Major General Keith Dayton of the Defense Intelligence Agency said, "Do I think we're going to find something? Yeah, I kind of do, because I think there's a lot of information out there."

—*Press Briefing, May 30, 2003*

PLANTED DEEP AND FULL OF MANURE

Family farms. Future Farmers of America. We've always heard that farming is the backbone of our country. We have images of the weather-beaten, heavily creased faces of farmers toiling in their fields and our eyes tear with pride. But in January 2002, the Associated Press reviewed the records of the U.S. Department of Agriculture and found out that more than 60 percent of federal farm subsidies went to just 10 percent of farmers, nearly all of them very wealthy. One recipient is a former pitcher for the Kansas City Royals, Kevin "Ape" Appier. Appier has received thousands of dollars in subsidies for his Kansas farm, which he purchased because his dream as a child was to play baseball and be a farmer. "I have no idea why I wanted to have a farm," he said. "I wasn't raised on a farm or anything. I just always thought it would be neat." Some of the other recipients of the federal handouts were farms owned by David Rockefeller, Ted Turner, Sam Donaldson, Enron's Kenneth Lay, and basketball legend Scottie Pippin. Seems like a lot of our tax money is going to a bunch of hoes.

"In my judgment, when the United States says there will be serious consequences, and if there isn't serious consequences, it creates adverse consequences."
—*George W. Bush,* Meet the Press, *February 8, 2004*

ALL YOU NEED IS LOVE

"It changes when you walk into a shut-in's house, and say, 'Can I love you?' or 'Can I help you?'"

—*George W. Bush, Trenton, New Jersey, September 23, 2002*

If you walk into a shut-in's house and say, "Can I love you?" you bet things will change—like the shape of your head or your arrest record.

"In order to defeat evil, you can do so by loving your neighbor like you'd like to be loved yourself."

—*George W. Bush, Port Elizabeth, New Jersey, June 24, 2002*

Of course loving your neighbor like you'd like to be loved yourself is only part of Bush's solution—the other part is bombing the crap out of a foreign country.

"I know they understand the proper role of government. And that is that government can't make people love one another."

—*George W. Bush, Philadelphia, Pennsylvania, March 12, 2002*

However, the government seems to have a great way of making people hate one another.

IN THE FISCAL YEAR 2003 FEDERAL BUDGET: $350,000 FOR SWEET POTATO RESEARCH.

NO INTELLIGENT LIFE ON THIS PLANET, CAPTAIN

It's easy to scam uneducated, naïve, and intellectually challenged people—that's why the United States Government is such an easy mark. A report issued by the United States Department of Energy in January 2002 revealed that federal facilities in Tennessee and Ohio actually tested a "Passive Magnetic Resonance Anomaly Mapping" (PMRAM) system. The PMRAM sounds very high-tech and intriguing but upon closer inspection it turns out to be nothing more than a fancy dowsing device. This device is worn on the wrist and is supposed to sense (through subtle changes in "magnetic field") underground faults, buried objects, water, and chemicals. It was reported that no one at either facility was skeptical about the device even after the contractor explained that there was only one "qualified" person in the world who could operate it, and he lived in the Ukraine. Someone might want to use that device to see if they can find these folks' brains.

"Yes, that's a—first of all, Mom, you're doing— that's tough. But it's—I appreciate that. I appreciate the idea of you wanting to give your children the education from you and the mom."
—*George W. Bush, Springfield, Missouri, February 9, 2004*

WHATEVER HAPPENS,
HAPPENS

"**Y**ou're going to be told lots of things. You get told things every day that don't happen. It doesn't seem to bother people, they don't— It's printed in the press. The world thinks all these things happen. They never happened. Everyone's so eager to get the story before in fact the story's there. That the world is constantly being fed things that haven't happened. All I can tell you is, it hasn't happened. It's going to happen."

—*Secretary of Defense Donald Rumsfeld,*
DOD Press Briefing, February 28, 2003

"And as I said in my State of the Union, the idea is to see that a car born today—I mean, a child born today will be driving a car, as his or her first car, which will be powered by hydrogen and pollution-free."
—*George W. Bush, Washington, D.C., February 6, 2003*

FORMER CIA DIRECTOR OUTED

President Bush awarded the nation's highest civilian honor, the Presidential Medal of Freedom, to former CIA Director George Tenet at a ceremony on December 14, 2004. Bush praised Tenet for improving the CIA (although he was director before and after the September 11, 2001, attacks) and lauded his rise from busboy at a diner in Queens, New York, to head of the CIA. With a straight face and no signs of malice, basically his smirking chimp look, President Bush proclaimed, "George is rightly—rightly proud of the people of the Agency, and I have been proud to work with George. George has carried great authority without putting on airs, because he remembers his roots. There's still a lotta Queens in George Tenet."

"I wasn't happy when we found out there wasn't weapons, and we've got an intelligence group together to figure out why."

—*George W. Bush, Second Presidential Debate, St. Louis, Missouri, October 8, 2004*

AVOIDANCE ISSUES

REPORTER: So when you say that you want the U.S. to adhere to international and U.S. laws, that's not very comforting. This is a moral question. Is terr—torture ever justified?

BUSH: Look, I'm gonna say it one more time. I can—if I can—maybe—maybe I can be more clear. The instructions went out to our people to adhere to law. That oughtta comfort you. We—we're a nation of law. We adhere to laws. We have laws on the books. You might look at those laws. And that might provide comfort for you. And those were the instructions out of—from me to the government.

—*Press Briefing, Savannah, Georgia, June 10, 2004*

Bush forgot one small detail; he never answered whether "torture" is "ever justified."

IN THE FISCAL YEAR 2005 FEDERAL BUDGET: $350,000 FOR THE ROCK AND ROLL HALL OF FAME IN CLEVELAND, OHIO (WHICH HAS RECEIVED $750,000 SINCE FISCAL 2002).

BUYER BEWARE

In order to keep the U.S. economy from sliding into a recession, the Federal Reserve reduces the interest rate to stimulate growth (during 2001 they did it a lot, remember?). "What is keeping us out of recession is the consumer," argues economist David Wyss of Standard & Poor's. "There is a risk of a sudden attack of prudence. If people stop living beyond their means, this could turn into a recession." So in other words, the only thing that is keeping our economy floating is the consumers' inability to control their spending. In that case—charge it!

"We're nearing the end of a year where—
of substantial progress at home and here abroad—
and abroad."

—*George W. Bush, Washington, D.C.,*
December 20, 2004

RANDOM BUSH

"**W**e can outcompete with anybody."
— *George W. Bush, Bay Shore, New York, March 11, 2004*

"**I**n terms of timetables, as quickly as possible—whatever that means."
— *George W. Bush, on his time frame for fixing Social Security,
Washington, D.C., March 16, 2005*

"**I** repeat, personal accounts do not permanently fix the solution."
— *George W. Bush, Washington, D.C., March 16, 2005*

"**I** want to appreciate those of you who wear our nation's uniform for your sacrifice."
— *George W. Bush, Jacksonville, Florida, January 14, 2005*

"**I** speak plainly sometimes, but you've got to be mindful of the consequences of the words. So put that down. I don't know if you'd call that a confession, a regret, something."
— *George W. Bush, speaking to reporters, Washington, D.C.,
January 14, 2005*

IN THE FISCAL YEAR 2004 FEDERAL BUDGET:
$302,500 FOR THE GRAVEYARD OF THE ATLANTIC
MUSEUM, A SHIPWRECK MUSEUM PLANNED FOR
HATTERAS ISLAND, NORTH CAROLINA.

HERE, PIGGY, PIGGY, PIGGY

While the symbol of our country, the Statue of Liberty, remains in desperate need of repair—it lacks the $5 million needed for upgrades—Congress still finds the money for more important projects including:

• $50 million to ensure that a Florida beach resort bridge remains toll-free
• $450,000 to study the DNA of rainbow trout
• $225,000 to repair a public swimming pool whose drain U.S. Representative Jim Gibbons (R-Nevada), as a child, clogged with tadpoles
• $40 million to the Port of Philadelphia for construction of a cargo terminal designed to support "high-speed military sealift and other military purposes." (Today, these types of vessels do not even exist, nor are they being championed by the military)
• $90,000 for the Cowgirl Hall of Fame
• $90,000 for fruit fly research in Montpellier, France
• $500,000 to the University of Akron for a project that analyzes how Congress makes difficult budget decisions.

I could save taxpayers that final $500,000 and let you know that Congress makes budget decisions based on how much pork members can bring home. I wonder if anyone's ever worked out the pork-for-votes exchange rate.

"Jessica Simpson is here with us, which means we've finally introduced reality TV to the Lincoln Theater."

—*George W. Bush, introducing the pop singer and reality TV star on March 14, 2004, at Ford's Theater in Washington, D.C. (Ford's Theater is where Lincoln was assassinated.)*

MR. KNOW-IT-ALL

"**I** think what you'll find, I think what you'll find is, whatever it is we do substantively, there will be near-perfect clarity as to what it is. And it will be known, and it will be known to the Congress, and it will be known to you, probably before we decide it, but it will be known."

—*Secretary of Defense Donald Rumsfeld, DOD Press Briefing, February 28, 2003*

I wish I knew what knowns he knows we know, you know?

"There's a gap between what he [John Kerry] promises and what he says he's going to do."

—*George W. Bush, Johnstown, Pennsylvania, September 9, 2004*

ACTUALLY, THERE IS NO GAP—"WHAT [JOHN KERRY] PROMISES" AND "WHAT HE SAYS HE'S GOING TO DO" MEAN THE SAME THING.

I'D LIKE TO THANK THE ACADEMY

In May 2002, the National Republican Congressional Committee named Covina City Council member Tom Palmeri "California Republican of the Year." The only problem with this honor is that Palmeri is a Democrat. He was sent a certificate and his name was listed along with 161 other honorees in a *Wall Street Journal* advertisement. Palmeri quickly learned his award came with a few strings attached. "All I keep getting is this bill for $150," he said. "And they'd like me to use my credit card." Palmeri was first honored a month earlier when a Republican fund-raising committee named him California Businessman of the Year.

"Too many good docs are getting out of the business. Too many OB/GYN's aren't able to practice their love with women all across the country."
—*George W. Bush, Poplar Bluff, Missouri, September 6, 2004*

THAT WOULD BE A REAL BLAST!

During the October 14, 2003, White House Press Briefing, Press Secretary Scott McClellan was confronted by Russell Mokhiber, editor of the *Corporate Crime Reporter*.

RUSSELL MOKHIBER: Scott, a couple things. Pat Robertson said this weekend that he wanted to nuke the State Department. The direct quote is, "If I could just get a nuclear device inside Foggy Bottom [the State Department's Washington headquarters], I think that's the answer. You've got to blow that thing up." Does the President have any reaction to that?

SCOTT MCCLELLAN: Yes. I think that, one, he has since said that he should not have said that and changed what he said. But I do not view those as helpful comments. And it was wrong for him to say that.

DAVID GREGORY NBC: That's it? Wait, wait.

SCOTT MCCLELLAN: No, no, those were harmful comments. He has now since said that he should not have said that.

DAVID GREGORY NBC: Can I follow up on Pat Robertson?

SCOTT MCCLELLAN: Go ahead.

DAVID GREGORY NBC: Will the President—besides not finding those comments helpful, I wonder if the President feels that he should have no involvement with Pat Robertson, whatever, going forward, and that Pat Robertson should

not play any role in any kind of unofficial way in helping him in reelection, in any kind of supportive role.

SCOTT MCCLELLAN: No, again—

DAVID GREGORY NBC: Would the President like Robertson to keep his distance?

SCOTT MCCLELLAN: Again, I think that those comments were harmful. And he, himself, said that he should not have said that. I think the comments were wrong, and he has since said so.

DAVID GREGORY NBC: So it's all forgiven?

I have a special message to Pat Robertson; Onward Christian soldiers doesn't mean they're armed with nuclear devices.

————◆————

"In this job you've got a lot on your plate on a regular basis; you don't have much time to sit around and wander, lonely, in the Oval Office, kind of asking different portraits, 'How do you think my standing will be?'"

—*George W. Bush, Washington, D.C., March 16, 2005*

I FEEL COMFORTED TO KNOW THAT BUSH REALIZES HE CAN'T SIT AROUND THE OVAL OFFICE AND TALK TO THE PAINTINGS.

FEED THE RICH

A congressional committee made public in May 2003 that five U.S. companies who relocated their headquarters offshore or overseas (as a way to avoid paying federal taxes) were still awarded nearly $1 billion in combined federal government contracts (our tax money).

Giving rise to the new phrase: "representation without taxation."

"The best way to describe it is, we're really happy with what we've seen so far. But we're realists in this administration. We understand that there's been years of hatred and distrust, and we'll continue to keep the process moving forward."

—*George W. Bush, Washington, D.C., July 2, 2003*

DID HE ACTUALLY SAY HE WAS GOING TO KEEP THE PROCESS OF HATRED AND DISTRUST MOVING FORWARD? WELL, HE'S DONE A FINE JOB SO FAR.

REALLY, IT'S JUST THAT SIMPLE

"Because the—all which is on the table begins to address the big cost drivers. For example, how benefits are calculated, for example, is on the table; whether or not benefits rise based upon wage increases or price increases. There's a series of parts of the formula that are being considered. And when you couple that, those different cost drivers, affecting those—changing those with personal accounts, the idea is to get what has been promised more likely to be—or closer delivered to what has been promised. Does that make any sense to you? It's kind of muddled. Look, there's a series of things that cause the—like, for example, benefits are calculated based upon the increase of wages, as opposed to the increase of prices. Some have suggested that we calculate—the benefits will rise based upon inflation, as opposed to wage increases. There is a reform that would help solve the red if that were put into effect. In other words, how fast benefits grow, how fast the promised benefits grow, if those—if that growth is affected, it will help on the red."

—*George W. Bush, explaining his plan to salvage Social Security, Tampa, Florida, February 4, 2005*

Now if someone will explain a plan to salvage his speech we might get somewhere.

"If they pre-decease or die early,
there's an asset base to be able to pass
on to a loved one."

—*George W. Bush, on private accounts for Social Security money,
Cedar Rapids, Iowa, March 30, 2005*

**DON'T YOU SIMPLY LOVE THE WORD
"PRE-DECEASE"?**

NOW YOU SEE IT, NOW YOU DON'T

In January 2003, the CIA brought together an open panel of scientists to discuss potential terrorist uses of life-science research. After much deliberation the panel agreed that, despite the risk, scientific research and study must remain open and available to the public to ensure advancement in these various fields. In April, the CIA stamped the panel's conclusions on openness as "Classified" and the report was sealed from public scrutiny.

"I think Jeb [Bush] and I were touched by what it means
to be sitting at a table with a daughter who has said,
I've got a responsibility to my mom."
—*George W. Bush, Miami, Florida, June 30, 2003*

I LOVE WHAT YOU'VE DONE
WITH THE PLACE

America's favorite blond, Jessica Simpson, toured the White House in March 2004. Simpson, who is known for making naïve, silly, or just plain idiotic remarks (i.e., "Isn't it plata-ma-pus? I always thought it was plata-ma-pus."), didn't disappoint her fans. While Jessica was looking around the White House she was introduced to Secretary of the Interior Gale Norton, to whom Simpson remarked, "You've done a nice job decorating the White House."

"I don't think there's a Democrat idea, I don't think it's a Republican idea, I think these are just ideas that need to be on the table. I think I'm the first President ever to have stood up and said, bring all your ideas forward."
—*George W. Bush, Cedar Rapids, Iowa, March 30, 2005*

I BET THAT MAKES THE FORTY-TWO FORMER PRESIDENTS FEEL PRETTY STUPID.

WORKING FOR SCALE

In October 2002, Acting Deputy Undersecretary of Defense for Equal Opportunity John M. Molino unveiled a novel way to alleviate the painful sounds of a sour note hit by a bugler playing "Taps" at military funerals. Working with private industry, the Department of Defense has created a device that fits deep into the bell of a bugle, and when a button is depressed, plays a "high-quality rendition of taps virtually indistinguishable from a live bugler." Even the most bungling bugler can now stride confidently onto the field and be assured of a groundbreaking performance.

"And I am an optimistic person. I guess if you want to try to find something to be pessimistic about, you can find it, no matter how hard you look, you know?"

—*George W. Bush, Washington, D.C., June 15, 2004*

A LOTT OF INCONSISTENCIES

"**H**ow dare Senator Daschle criticize President Bush while we are fighting our war on terrorism, especially when we have troops in the field!"

—Trent Lott, February 28, 2002

"**I** cannot support this military action in the Persian Gulf at this time. Both the timing and the policy are subject to question."

—Trent Lott, criticizing President Clinton during Operation Desert Fox when we had troops in the field, December 1998

"I want to thank the astronauts who are with us, the courageous spacial entrepreneurs who set such a wonderful example for the young of our country."

—George W. Bush, Washington, D.C., January 14, 2004

"SPACIAL ENTREPRENEURS?"

CHECK YOUR FACTS

During the vice presidential debates in 2004, Senator John Edwards questioned Vice President Dick Cheney about his role at Halliburton. The Vice President responded by suggesting people log on to their computers and click over to the Annenberg Public Policy Center of the University of Pennsylvania. But when Cheney was giving out the URL he said factcheck.com instead of the correct site name, factcheck.org. When people went to the .com site they were redirected to GeorgeSoros.com, which bore the headline, "Why we must not re-elect President Bush." Thanks to Cheney's mis.com.munication the site saw nearly fifty thousand visitors the first hour, up from two hundred visits the previous day.

"And I'm back in the same old job. I feel like a gerbil.
I get up every morning, run like the dickens,
and I stay right where I am."
— *Secretary of Defense Donald Rumsfeld,*
Fort Campbell, Kentucky, September 14, 2004

PREACHING TO THE CHOIR

"**T**his amendment would destroy the best drug court system in the country. It would require that first-and second-time offenders, irrespective of what their crime was, be given treatment. What the drug court does is provide services, but also says there's a consequence."

> —*Florida Governor Jeb Bush, addressing forty-five*
> *graduates of Miami-Dade County's drug court*
> *on May 17, 2002*

Bush was referring to a ballot proposition misleadingly called, "A Right to Treatment," which, as written, would hamper the drug courts and make drug treatment less effective. For his part, Governor Bush has increased substance-abuse treatment and prevention by 62 percent or $95 million. Under Governor Bush, over 45,000 additional people have entered drug treatment programs for a total of 245,000 people receiving treatment in 2001. You've got to hand it to the guy, he's definitely got drugs on his mind. Of course Jeb has some first-hand knowledge of drugs. In January 2002, his daughter Noelle was arrested on charges of trying to buy the antianxiety drug Xanax with a fake ID and was sentenced to a treatment program instead of jail time. But while she was in the

treatment center, she was found to be in possession of an unauthorized prescription medicine and was sentenced to three days in jail (July 2002). After jail she went back to the treatment center where she was arrested in September 2002 for buying crack cocaine, which rehab staff members found in her shoe.

"If only I could have heard Johnny Mathis sing,
then I would have wished Laura were here again."
—*George W. Bush, Los Angeles, California, June 27, 2003*

BOMBS AWAY

The Pentagon is trying to calm the fears of people who live on the coast of Georgia by claiming that what they lost there in 1958 is safe and isn't a threat. What the Pentagon lost somewhere in the ocean on February 5, 1958, is just a 3,450 kg hydrogen bomb. It was jettisoned from a damaged B-47 Stratojet bomber during a training exercise, and its exact whereabouts is unknown. The Pentagon assured citizens that the bomb is safe because the detonator had been removed, but recently discovered documents revealing that the bomb is armed. The mayor of the city of Tybee Island, Georgia, summed it up best by stating: "It's in the best interest of everybody that it be found to determine what condition the weapon is in."

"And so during these holiday seasons,
we thank our blessings ..."
—*George W. Bush, Fort Belvoir, Virginia, December 10, 2004*

HERE COME DA JUDGE

The City Club in Cleveland, Ohio, which routinely hosts appearances by public figures, awarded Supreme Court Justice Antonin Scalia its Citadel of Free Speech Award in March 2005. The award recognizes Scalia because he has "consistently, across the board, had opinions or led the charge in support of free speech." A proclamation honored Scalia for protecting free speech in several Supreme Court cases, including voting against the controversial Texas flag-burning ban. "Justice Scalia has consistently demonstrated a commitment to the values of free speech where it counts most: protecting the speech of those whose views we disagree with most," the proclamation reads. So why didn't we hear more about Scalia's award for championing free speech? Because Scalia banned television and radio coverage as a condition of his appearance. This crusader of free speech also doesn't allow recording devices of any kind in the Supreme Court chamber.

"And, obviously, the more help we can get, the more we appreciate it. And we are continuing to work with other nations to ask their help advice."
—*George W. Bush, Crawford, Texas, July 21, 2003*

"HELP ADVICE"? ANYONE KNOW WHAT THAT MEANS?

LAST ONE THERE IS A ROTTEN EGG

When the presidents were announced at the opening of the Clinton Presidential Center in Arkansas, President Bush physically pushed former President Bill Clinton aside so he could get through the library door first (see photo at www.RealWacky.com). During the course of the day Bush's behavior remained passive-aggressive; like this exchange made to a tour guide as they looked at the Arkansas River.

TOUR GUIDE: Usually, you might see some bass fishermen out there.

GEORGE BUSH: A submarine could take this place out.

To show his support for Clinton, Bush had agreed to attend the entire ceremony, but at the private luncheon, which took place in a heated tent pitched behind the library, Bush was gone even before Shimon Peres gave his toast to the former President.

"I'm not into this detail stuff. I'm more concepty."

—*Secretary of Defense Donald Rumsfeld,*
the New Yorker, *June 17, 2002*

DON'T KNOW IF WE'RE COMING OR GOING

"It breaks my heart to see the loss of innocent life and to see brave troops in combat lose their life. It just breaks my heart. But I understand what's going on. These people are trying to shake the will of the Iraqi citizens, and they want us to leave. That's what they want us to do. And I think the world would be better off if we did leave. If we didn't—if we left, the world would be worse."

—George W. Bush, Derry, New Hampshire, September 20, 2004

Nearly half of the people in the United States thinks he said it right the first time and the other half thinks he said it right the second time.

"Our productivity is high. I hope some of it has to do— I know some of it has to do, I hope you understand some of it has to do with the fact that the role of government can help create growth."

—George W. Bush, Halethorpe, Maryland, December 5, 2003

FLOWER POWER

Floriculture is one of the rapidly expanding segments in Hawaii's agricultural industry: in 2002, its wholesale value in Hawaii reached $92.1 million. So why did Congress dole out $355,000 for Hawaiian floriculture research in 2005? Because Senate appropriator Daniel Inouye (D-Hawaii) knows the sweet smell of pork. Inouye is responsible for Hawaii being in second place in order of states that receive the greatest amount of federal dollars per capita (Alaska is number one).

"The best way to protect us is to stay on the offensive and to find terrorists before they try to harm us again. And they will."
—*George W. Bush, Nashua, New Hampshire, March 25, 2004*

MORE RANDOM BUSH

"**I** believe we are called to do the hard work to make our communities and quality of life a better place."

—*George W. Bush, Collinsville, Illinois, January 5, 2005*

"**W**hen a drug comes in from Canada, I wanna make sure it cures ya, not kill ya . . . I've got an obligation to make sure our government does everything we can to protect you. And one—my worry is that it looks like it's from Canada, and it might be from a third world."

—*George W. Bush, Second Presidential Debate,*
St. Louis, Missouri, October 8, 2004

"**W**e all thought there was weapons there, Robin. My opponent thought there was weapons there."

—*George W. Bush, Second Presidential Debate,*
St. Louis, Missouri, October 8, 2004

"**L**et me see where to start here. First, the *National Journal* named Senator Kennedy the most liberal senator of all."

—*George W. Bush, referring to Senator Kerry, Second Presidential*
Debate, St. Louis, Missouri, October 8, 2004

"**I** saw a poll that said the right track/wrong track in Iraq was better than here in America. It's pretty darn strong. I mean, the people see a better future."

—*George W. Bush, Washington, D.C., September 23, 2004*

IN THE FISCAL YEAR 2002 FEDERAL BUDGET: $600,000 TO RESEARCH THE SEX LIFE OF THE SOUTH AFRICAN GROUND SQUIRREL.

AN OPENED AND CLOSED CASE

In 2001, the U.S. Food and Drug Administration endorsed the approval of a unique implantable device designed to prevent uncontrollable bowel movements. The invention imitates the function of the sphincter muscle and basically helps keep your trap shut. Patients who have received successful implants seemed to experience a dramatic improvement in their quality of life (and so do the people they live with).

> "After standing on the stage, after the debates, I made it very plain, we will not have an all-volunteer army. And yet, this week—we will have an all-volunteer army. Let me restate that."
> —*George W. Bush, Daytona Beach, Florida, October 16, 2004*

HE'S SUCH A GOOD LITTLE BOY

REPORTER: "Sir, there's a widespread perception in this town that when it comes to the Iraqis and the Palestinians, you are a hard-liner. Are you comfortable with that? [Laughter] And—"

DONALD RUMSFELD: "Look at me! I'm sweet and lovable."

—Secretary of Defense Donald Rumsfeld, Foreign Press Center, June 2, 2002

"What we don't know yet is what we thought and what the Iraqi Survey Group has found, and we want to look at that."

—George W. Bush, Washington, D.C., February 2, 2004

I LOVE YOU, YOU LOVE ME!

"**T**hey can't take it. If you play it for twenty-four hours, your brain and body functions start to slide, your train of thought slows down and your will is broken. That's when we come in and talk to them," Sergeant Mark Hadsell of the United States Psychological Operations Company (Psy Ops) said. He is talking about the military's prolonged playing of music that is culturally offensive to prisoners in order to break down their will. So what's on the hit list of disturbing music? Sergeant Hadsell's favorites are "Bodies" from the XXX film soundtrack and Metallica's "Enter Sandman." Other torturous music is the theme song from *Sesame Street* and songs from the dancing, singing, purple dinosaur, Barney. However, the human rights organization, Amnesty International, said such tactics may constitute torture, and U.S. and coalition forces could be in breach of the Geneva Convention. I tend to agree with Amnesty International—as a parent I think listening to music from Barney is torture!

"There's no doubt in my mind that we should allow the world's worst leaders to hold America hostage, to threaten our peace, to threaten our friends and allies with the world's worst weapons."
—*George W. Bush, South Bend, Indiana, September 5, 2002*

"WE ENDED THE RULE OF
ONE OF HISTORY'S
WORST TYRANTS,
AND IN SO DOING, WE NOT ONLY
FREED THE AMERICAN PEOPLE,
WE MADE
OUR OWN PEOPLE
MORE SECURE."

—*George W. Bush, Crawford, Texas, May 3, 2003*

I SPY WITH MY LITTLE EYE

During an inspection tour President Bush took the opportunity to observe the surroundings through a pair of binoculars. The only problem is that he forgot to take off the lens caps. Military personnel have verified that these are standard binoculars and not the fancy night-vision glasses (that have little holes in the lens covers to prevent damage from sunlight). Sounds like someone else might have had too much exposure to the sun.

THE PRESIDENT'S NIECE, LAUREN BUSH, APPEARED ON THE APRIL 2002 COVER OF *W* MAGAZINE. THE ACCOMPANYING CAPTION FOR THE PHOTOGRAPH READ: BURNING BUSH: LAUREN BUSH HEATS UP.

"ON THE TAX CUT,
IT'S A BIG DECISION.

THE RIGHT DECISION."

—*George W. Bush, Second Presidential Debate,*
St. Louis, Missouri, October 8, 2004

THEIR BOSS IS A REAL DICK!

During the 2002 Olympics in Salt Lake City, Utah, Secret Service agents entered a skateboard and apparel shop near the Rice-Eccles Stadium, where the closing ceremony was held, and purchased an Olympic hat. They paid the clerk the $11 for the hat and then left a big tip—or a tip-off. The agents inadvertently left a document detailing security plans for Vice President Dick Cheney's appearance at the closing ceremony. The document, titled "Site Post Assignment Log," described seating arrangements for Cheney, his wife and daughter, and other dignitaries. It also had the itinerary for various locations that Cheney would visit during the day, the number of Secret Service agents on duty, where they would be stationed, and their specific assignments. It revealed as well the "sweep time" (when agents search the stadium for weapons, bombs, unauthorized people, etc., before the VP's arrival). The owner reported the mistake to a Secret Service representative who promised agents would be there immediately to retrieve the document. After forty-five minutes, no one had arrived, so the owner took the document to the agency's downtown office. In return for being a good citizen the man requested the Vice President's autograph. He was refused. But instead of getting mad, he got even and went to the newspaper with the story.

———————◆———————

IN THE FISCAL YEAR 2005
FEDERAL BUDGET:
$1 MILLION WAS EARMARKED TO
RESTORE WOODY ISLAND AND
HISTORIC STRUCTURES IN ALASKA.
ACCORDING TO ALASKA'S
DEPARTMENT OF COMMERCE
WEB SITE, WOODY ISLAND HAS AN
OFFICIAL POPULATION OF "0"
AND IS OCCUPIED ONLY ON A
SEASONAL BASIS.

SPOCK, YOU AND YOUR DAMN LOGIC!

"**Y**ou know, there's concern about jobs going overseas. I share the concern. We want people working here. We want our jobs here. And the best way to do so is to make sure this is the best place to do business in the world. The best way to make sure jobs are here, this is a place for risk-takers, feel comfortable taking risk, and you're able to do so without getting sued right and left—so we need tort reform."

—*George W. Bush, Hudson, Wisconsin, August 18, 2004*

A perfect example of Bush taking a huge logical leap to the right by attributing the cause of outsourcing overseas to companies that fear being sued, and coming up with the answer—tort reform.

In 2003, the CIA asked *Alias* star Jennifer Garner to appear in its recruiting video. "Her participation would add a human touch," said a spokesperson for the CIA.

NOW YOU GUYS KNOW SHE'S NOT A REAL AGENT, DON'T YOU?

WORD SCRAMBLE

REPORTER: Thank you, Mr. President. You do have now the personal gun of Saddam Hussein. Are you willing to give it to President Al-Yawar as a symbolic gift, or are you keeping it?

BUSH: What she's referring to is a—members of a Delta team came to see me in the Oval Office and brought with me—these were the people that found Saddam Hussein, the dictator of Iraq, hiding in a hole. And, by the way, let me remind everybody about Saddam Hussein, just in case we all forget. There were mass graves under his leadership. There were torture chambers. Saddam Hussein—if you—we had seven people come to my office. Perhaps the foreign press didn't see this story. Seven people came to my—they had their hands cut off because the Iraqi currency had devalued. And Saddam Hussein needed somebody to blame, so he blamed small merchants. And their hands were chopped off, their right hand.

—Savannah, Georgia, June 10, 2004

Just in case you were wondering, Bush never got back to the question regarding gifting the confiscated gun to President Al-Yawar. Is it just me or does reading that paragraph make you dizzy?

IN THE FISCAL YEAR 2005 FEDERAL BUDGET: $500,000 FOR THE INSTITUTE FOR FURNITURE MANUFACTURING AND MANAGEMENT AT MISSISSIPPI STATE UNIVERSITY.

BUSH-HOG!

An article in the *Boston Globe* (September 5, 2002) reported that then gubernatorial candidate, now Governor Mitt Romney (R-Massachusetts), speaking before business leaders, recalled a conversation with President Bush during the opening ceremony of the Olympics: "The television audience was estimated at 3.5 billion, more than half the population of the planet. And I'm standing next to the President of the United States, and what I thought to myself is, when we go out there, what does he think? You know what, the President of the United States, as he goes out to an audience like that, with three and a half billion people looking at him, he turned to me and he said, 'Do I look fat?'"

I wonder if Bush feels self-conscious every time he walks into the Rotunda Room?

REPORTER FOR THE *WASHINGTON POST*: Why do you think bin Laden has not been caught?

GEORGE BUSH: Because he's hiding.

—George W. Bush, in an interview with Michael A. Fletcher and Jim VandeHei of the Washington Post, *aboard* Air Force One, *January 14, 2005*

HIDE AND GO SEEK

Here is Secretary of Defense Donald Rumsfeld discussing inspectors visiting Iraq in search of weapons of mass destruction and how some congressmen, desperate for a photo op, have gone (on taxpayer money, of course) to look for the weapons, as well.

"So they allow inspectors in at times of their convenience and their choosing and have hidden things. They have things that are mobile; they have things that are underground. It is next to impossible with a group of people like that who have spent years digging underground for a handful of—I can't think of anything funnier than a handful of congressmen wandering around thinking—you've seen the size of the country? They'd have to be there for the next fifty years trying to find something. [Laughter] I mean, it's a joke."

—Secretary of Defense Donald Rumsfeld, interview with
the National Journalists Roundtable, August 5, 2002

It's comforting to know that Rumsfeld's opinion of Congress is pretty much the same as that of most people in the United States. But on the plus side, a handful of congressmen staying in Iraq for fifty years is a good start.

"I'm never disappointed in my Secretary of Defense.
He's doing a fabulous job, and America is lucky to
have him in the position he's in."

—George W. Bush, Washington, D.C., June 17, 2004

·157·

A STEERING COMMITTEE

The *Washington Post* reported in 2003 that Washington, D.C., Maryland, and Virginia spent $1.64 million in federal funds (your tax dollars) to install bike racks on every single Metro bus. The rationale was to provide more incentive for people to use bikes and public transportation to commute to work. According to the article, of the estimated 85,000 daily trips in the Washington, D.C., area, bicycles do less than 1 percent, with three-fourths of that number representing people running errands or biking for recreation. Looks like Congress just can't put the brakes on their cycle of spending.

"Government should be an advocate of faith-based and community-based programs, not an *impedent* to faith-based programs. Government ought to be not a road block."
—*George W. Bush, Washington, D.C., April 1, 2005*

AND THE PRESIDENT OUGHT TO NOT MAKE UP WORDS.

YOU BETTER HIGHTAIL IT OUT OF HERE, PILGRIM

On July 2, 2003, in Washington, D.C., President Bush had this gung-ho comment to make about American troops being in harm's way in Iraq.

"There are some who feel like that, uhh—if they—attack us, that we may decide to leave prematurely. They don't understand what they're talkin' about, if that's the case. Let me finish. Umm, there are some who, uhh—feel like—that, you know, the conditions are such that they can attack us there. My answer is bring 'em on."

After getting criticized for his John Wayne attitude when it comes to the lives of the men and women he sent overseas, Bush tried to backpedal out of the comment.

"Sometimes, words have consequences you don't intend them to mean. 'Bring 'em on' is the classic example, when I was really trying to rally the troops and make it clear to them that I fully understood, you know, what a great job they were doing. And those words had an unintended consequence.

It kind of, some interpreted it to be defiance in the face of danger. That certainly wasn't the case."
—*George W. Bush, Washington, D.C., January 14, 2005*

Maybe I'm wrong, but doesn't it seem a little irresponsible for someone who's not in the line of fire to act so cavalierly when there are people's lives at stake?

"As you know, we don't have relationships with Iran. I mean, that's—ever since the late '70s, we have no contacts with them, and we've totally sanctioned them. In other words, there's no sanctions—you can't— we're out of sanctions."
—*George W. Bush, Annandale, Virginia, August 9, 2004*

EXCEPT FOR THAT INSIGNIFICANT LITTLE TIME BETWEEN 1980 AND 1988 WHEN WE COVERTLY SOLD ARMS TO IRAN (AKA THE IRAN-CONTRA AFFAIR) DURING THEIR BLOODY CONFRONTATION WITH IRAQ.

LET ME INTRODUCE TO YOU, THE ONE AND ONLY BILLY SHEARS

Entomologists Quentin Wheeler and Kelly Miller discovered sixty-five new species of slime-mold beetles (published in the March 24, 2005, issue of the *Bulletin of the American Museum of Natural History*) and decided to name three of them after the President, the Vice President, and the Secretary of Defense. Roll out the red carpet for: *Agathidium bushi Miller and Wheeler, Agathidium cheneyi Miller and Wheeler,* and *Agathidium rumsfeldi Miller and Wheeler* (First word is the genus, the second word must end in an "i" if it's named after someone, and the last part reflects the person[s] who first described the species). Wheeler and Miller claim they named the bugs as an homage to the three politicians. "We admire these leaders as fellow citizens who have the courage of their convictions and are willing to do the very difficult and unpopular work of living up to principles of freedom and democracy rather than accepting the expedient or popular," Wheeler said.

IN THE FISCAL YEAR 2004 FEDERAL BUDGET: $1.5 MILLION FOR THE MONTANA STATE UNIVERSITY, BOZEMAN, MONTANA, FOR THE CENTER FOR STUDYING LIFE IN EXTREME ENVIRONMENTS.

PRESTO CHANGO!

BUSH: How old is your child, Carl?

CARL: Fourteen years old.

BUSH: Yes, fourteen. Well, if she were—

CARL: He, sir.

BUSH: He, excuse me. I should have done the background check.
She will—when she gets ready to—when she's fifty, the
system will be broke, if my math is correct.

—*Washington, D.C., January 26, 2005*

I don't think I would be worrying about my math when my
short-term memory was in such bad shape.

Speaking of memory loss, at a press briefing on
June 24, 2003, Defense Secretary Donald Rumsfeld declared:
"I don't know anybody that I can think of who has contended
that the Iraqis had nuclear weapons."

TAKE A BOW

When Condoleezza Rice cruised into the Bush Cabinet, people wondered where this powerhouse woman came from. In 1991, Condoleezza Rice was named a director for the Chevron Corporation and was obviously well liked because in 1995 Chevron named its largest oil tanker (136,000 tons) the *Condoleezza Rice.* Now I'm not sure how flattering it is to a woman to have a huge, bulky, floating oil barrel named for her, but it's the thought that counts. Anyway, once Condi started working for Bush as his National Security Adviser on January 22, 2001, I suppose it didn't seem appropriate to have a tanker floating around with her name on it (imagine the headlines if it sprang a leak). In May 2001, Chevron changed the name of the tanker to *Altair Voyager* because, as Chevron's Fred Gorell said, "We made the change to eliminate unnecessary attention caused by the vessel's original name."

And to eliminate all the late-night talk show jokes.

◆

"The deficit is less than we thought because the revenues is exceeding projections. And the reason why the revenues —the revenues are exceeding projections— sometimes I mangle the English language. I get that."
—*George W. Bush, Washington, D.C., November 4, 2004*

ADRIFT IN A SEA OF CONFUSION

"**I**'ll give you an interesting idea that took place in Maine. They've got Maine lobstermen [who] are now patrolling the coast on a volunteer basis to make sure that somebody in a—somebody carrying something they don't want to carry in a boat shows up on the coast. I mean, there's all kinds of ways to serve the community."
—*George W. Bush, Daytona Beach, Florida, January 30, 2002*

Speaking of boats: I wonder if Bush got confused when someone told him Condoleezza Rice used to be an oil tanker.

IN JULY 2004, THE ENVIRONMENTAL PROTECTION AGENCY'S (EPA) LEAK-SAFETY STANDARDS FOR THE NUCLEAR WASTE REPOSITORY AT NEVADA'S YUCCA MOUNTAIN WERE REJECTED BY A FEDERAL APPEALS COURT. THE EPA HAD REPORTED THAT THE PROPOSED SITE WAS SAFE UNTIL THE YEAR A.D. 12,000, BUT THE COURT SAID THAT WAS TOO CLOSE FOR COMFORT. THEY CITED A NATIONAL ACADEMY OF SCIENCES REPORT THAT RECOMMENDED PROTECTION UNTIL THE YEAR A.D. 302,000.

ONE MORE TIME FOR OLD TIMES' SAKE

During his State of the Union speech, President Bush unbelievably hung on to the Weapons of Mass Destruction excuse for invading Iraq. Instead of admitting that no report issued and not a single investigation to date has turned up weapons, he tried one more time to WMD us:

"We are seeking all the facts. Already the Kay Report identified dozens of *weapons of mass destruction-related program activities* and significant amounts of equipment that Iraq concealed from the United Nations. Had we failed to act, the dictator's weapons of mass destruction programs would continue to this day."

—George W. Bush, State of the Union address,
Washington, D.C., January 21, 2004

He's not saying they found weapons of mass destruction, nor is he saying they found proof of weapons of mass destruction programs, he's saying they found weapons of mass destruction-related program activities—but never explains what those are . . . and how they justified invading another country.

"Alphonso and I have set a job. We want to close the minority homeownership gap in America. We want more people owning their own home, and we want more of our minorities owning their own home, as well."
—George W. Bush, Ardmore, Pennsylvania, March 15, 2004

MAKING THE DISTINCTION BETWEEN PEOPLE AND MINORITIES.

AIN'T THAT ANOTHER NAME
FOR A NEEDLE?

REPORTER: On Iraq, can the American people expect that by the end of your first term you will have effected a regime change in Iraq, one way or another? And by the same token—

BUSH: That's hypothetical.

REPORTER: But can the American people expect that? Should they expect that?

BUSH: That's a hypothetical question. They can expect me not to answer hypothetical questions.

REPORTER: On Osama bin Laden does your promise still—

BUSH: On sensitive subjects. [Laughter]

REPORTER: Sir, on Osama bin Laden, does your promise still hold that he will be caught, dead or alive, at some point?

BUSH: What? Say that again?

REPORTER: Does your promise on—or your goal of catching Osama bin Laden dead or alive, does that still stand?

BUSH: I don't know if he is dead or alive, for starters — so I'm going to answer your question with a hypothetical. Osama bin Laden, he may be alive. If he is, we'll get him. If he's not alive, we got him.

—Washington D.C., July 8, 2002

Bush seems to have a shaky concept of what the word "hypothetical" means—especially when he answers the reporter's question with his own "hypothetical." If, however, he thinks the word means "I don't want to answer your question" then he's using it correctly.

"By the way, 'to whom much has been given, much is owed.' Not only are we leading the world in terms of encouraging freedom and peace, we're feeding the hungry. We're taking care of, as best as we possibly can, the victims of HIV/AIDS."

—*George W. Bush, Cedar Rapids, Iowa, July 20, 2004*

IN THIS PASSAGE, BUSH SHOWS OFF HIS REBORN CHRISTIAN PERSONA BY ATTEMPTING TO QUOTE SCRIPTURE (LUKE 12:48—"TO WHOM MUCH IS GIVEN, MUCH IS *REQUIRED*."), EXCEPT THE APOSTLE GEORGE'S VERSION MEANS THE EXACT OPPOSITE.

THE MONEY PIT

Senate appropriator Kay Bailey Hutchison (R-Texas) earmarked $3 million for the North Padre Island Packery Channel project. Added into the Fiscal Year 2004 Federal Budget, the plans for this massive Texas project involve dredging a channel through a popular beach on the island. This would link the Laguna Madre to the Gulf of Mexico via the Packery Channel and require 30 million taxpayer dollars to complete. After spending this huge amount of our money, developers will be able to take advantage of the newly transformed part of the barrier island and turn it into a resort (complete with beachside hotels, shops, restaurants, a golf course, amusement park, and more). According to the *Amarillo Globe News,* "Scientists and residents said the new project would benefit only a handful of wealthy [North Padre Island, Texas] residents." Since 2001, taxpayers have contributed $8,836,000 to this Texas resort destination. So if you're ever in North Padre Island, Texas, stop by this lovely resort, play a round of golf, have a bite to eat, and visit your money.

"[Arkansas and Alabama] don't need fancy theories, or what may sound good. Science is not an art—I mean, reading is not an art. It's a science. We know what works."
—*George W. Bush, Washington, D.C., September 4, 2002*

I'M NOT BILINGUAL—I JUST LIKE GIRLS

GREGORY: I wonder why it is you think there are such strong sentiments in Europe against you and against this administration? Why, particularly, there's a view that you and your administration are trying to impose America's will on the rest of the world, particularly when it comes to the Middle East and where the war on terrorism goes next? [In French to President Chirac:] And, Mr. President, would you maybe comment on that?

BUSH: Very good. The guy memorizes four words, and he plays like he's intercontinental.

GREGORY: I can go on.

BUSH: I'm impressed—que bueno. Now I'm literate in two languages.

—*George W. Bush and David Gregory, Paris, France, May 26, 2002*

Bush answers NBC White House correspondent David Gregory's question by trying to insult him while Gregory was graciously addressing French President Jacques Chirac in his own language.

"Once in a while, I'm standing here, doing something. And I think, 'What in the world am I doing here?' It's a big surprise."

—*Secretary of Defense Donald Rumsfeld, interview with the* New York Times, *May 16, 2001*

A GAY OLD TIME

At the close of the July 2, 2004, meeting of the Association of
Southeast Asian Nations (ASEAN) Regional Forum in Jakarta,
Indonesia, Secretary of State Colin Powell took the stage with five
other U.S. officials. Were they there to give a speech or talk about
diplomatic relationships with Southeast Asia and the United
States? No, they were there to sing. Powell, decked out in a hard
hat with a hammer stuck in his belt, sang a parody of the Village
People's hit "YMCA" as the construction worker. The other officials sang backup and discoed the night away as Colin sang lyrics
like: "President Bush, he said to me, Colin, I need you to run the
department of state. We are between a rock and a hard place."

"Who could have possibly envisioned an erection—
an election in Iraq at this point in history?"
—*George W. Bush, Washington, D.C., January 10, 2005*

TAX FACTS

"**O**ne of the worst taxes—one of the worst taxes in America is what they call the death tax. It's a tax that taxes people's assets more than once. It's a tax that hurts farmers and ranchers. It says you cannot leave your business—if you're a small business owner—to your relative."

— *George W. Bush, Minneapolis, Minnesota, July 11, 2002*

Actually, it's only called the "death tax" by its detractors; the real name is the Estate Tax or Inheritance Tax. Also, the tax doesn't say you cannot leave your business to relatives, but rather says the beneficiary is required to pay tax on what they receive.

**IN THE FISCAL YEAR 2002 FEDERAL BUDGET:
$273,000 FOR BLUE SPRINGS, MISSOURI,
TO FIGHT THE INVASION OF "GOTH"
CULTURE AMONG ITS YOUNG.**

TILL YOU'RE BLUE IN THE FACE

The University of Maine received $2.7 million for a research project on low-bush blueberries. Low-bush blueberries are not grown on farms but are actually common forest ground-cover plants. It seems like Mother Nature has done all the work so why are taxpayers' pockets being picked? Two reasons, Republican Senators Susan Collins and Olympia Snowe, and their ability to plant the blueberry research in the budget. But the roots of this blueberry bounty runs deep; in 2002, Congress served up $10 million for blueberry purchases. According to a 2002 *Wall Street Journal* article, the $10 million would be about 12 million pounds of wild blueberries—and that works out to be between 16 and 17 percent of the entire annual industry crop. "Why all the fuss for a fruit that sells at a premium and that grows naturally throughout New England, New York, and elsewhere?" asked the *Journal*. "Politicians, of course," who "love to harvest the federal government's bounty for home-state farmers." So the blueberry industry in Maine gets a $12 million slice of the federal pie and the rest of the United States can kiss their muffins.

"After all, Europe is America's closest ally."
—*George W. Bush, Mainz, Germany, February 23, 2005*

TRIMMING THE BUSH

"It doesn't make any sense to have a forest policy that will not allow for thinning and clearing, a forest policy that is so backward that we allow kindling to build up in these forests, and then with an act of nature, or with a sleight of hand by mankind, our national treasures burn to the ground."

—*George W. Bush, Northern State University, Aberdeen, South Dakota, October 31, 2002*

In the name of fire prevention (in his mind trees are kindling and need to be cleared), Bush wants to allow the timber industry to log off more than 2.5 million acres of federal forest over the next ten years. So basically, it's a huge federal giveaway program to benefit big timber companies.

IN THE FISCAL YEAR 2004 FEDERAL BUDGET: $270,000 FOR POTATO STORAGE RESEARCH AT THE AGRICULTURE RESEARCH SERVICE LABORATORY IN MADISON, WISCONSIN.

JENNA AND TONIC

Just two weeks after President Bush's nineteen-year-old daughter Jenna Bush was cited for underage drinking, she and her twin sister Barbara were caught trying to buy alcohol at a popular Austin restaurant called Chuy's. On May 29, 2001, Jenna attempted to purchase a beer, and when asked for identification, produced someone else's driver's license. The manager, Mia Lawrence, who was either a Democrat or afraid the beer would kill Jenna, called 911 to report the incident.

"I'm trying to put a leash on 'em."

—*George W. Bush, explaining how he plans to deal with his daughters' behavior, First Presidential Debate, Coral Gables, Florida, September 30, 2004*

IF YOU CAN'T DAZZLE THEM
WITH BRILLIANCE . . .

"**S**o that is what we're doing and trying to do and it creates tensions in any institution when you do that. People get attracted and attached to what is and they know about it and they're comfortable with it and they don't want to give it up and they'd like a few more of them, as opposed to being willing to take some of the funds for that and stick it into investments for something that will not really benefit this country until after their careers are over and certainly long after I'm gone at my age."

—Secretary of Defense Donald Rumsfeld, interview with the
National Journalists Roundtable, August 5, 2002

I've decided to enter this quote in the "World's Longest Sentence" contest.

IN 2003, THE U.S. SENATE BEGAN INTENSE
DELIBERATIONS OVER PRESIDENT BUSH'S
TAX BILL—UNTIL IT CAME TO THE ATTENTION
OF ONE MEMBER THAT THEY WERE DEBATING
THE WRONG BILL.

TO BEE OR NOT TO BEE

Officials at the Pentagon announced in May 2002 that they had successfully trained bees to sniff out explosives. "It appears bees are at least as sensitive or more sensitive to odors than dogs," says Dr. Alan Rudolph, who is overseeing the sting operation. The report explained that only one bee in a hive need be trained (finding explosives equals sugar water). The trained bee will forward that information to other bees in the hive and, literally within hours, the entire hive will know the benefits of discovering explosives. Officials admit that the plan has several drawbacks; one, it has an enormous "giggle factor" and two, bees have limitations such as not being able to work at night or in cold weather.

Sounds like most federal employees to me.

IN THE FISCAL YEAR 2003 FEDERAL BUDGET:
$4 MILLION FOR THE INTERNATIONAL FERTILIZER
DEVELOPMENT CENTER (IFDC) IN ALABAMA.

IN THE FISCAL YEAR 2004 AND 2005 FEDERAL BUDGETS:
$1.7 MILLION (PER YEAR) FOR THE INTERNATIONAL
FERTILIZER DEVELOPMENT CENTER IN ALABAMA.

SINCE 1997, CONGRESS HAS DUMPED $15.7 MILLION INTO
THE IFDC PROGRAM—THE ONLY THING MORE FULL OF
FERTILIZER THAN THIS PROGRAM IS CONGRESS.

FONDUES AND FON-DON'TS

BUSH: Is everybody enjoying themselves here?
REPORTER: I only just got here, so . . .
BUSH: Yes, I know. Where have you been?
REPORTER: Sucking up the salt air on the West Coast.
BUSH: Brie and cheese?
REPORTER: No, tennis.

—*Crawford, Texas, August 23, 2001*

Although he wasn't very Gouda at it, Bush was trying to make an elitist joke at a reporter's expense only to have the remark backfire on him.

ACCORDING TO THE WATCHDOG GROUP, CITIZENS AGAINST GOVERNMENT WASTE, IN FISCAL YEAR 2001, THERE WAS $18.5 BILLION IN PORK-BARREL SPENDING. AT THE SAME TIME PENTAGON OFFICIALS PREDICTED AN $18 BILLION SHORTFALL IN THE DEFENSE BUDGET TO FIGHT THE WAR ON TERRORISM.

THE CONGRESSIONAL
FIVE-FINGER DISCOUNT

In July 2003, the U.S. Senate Rules Committee considered adopting a new rule (because that's what they do) that senators cannot steal historical artifacts from the U.S. Capitol. "We're not supposed to, but it has been a regular practice over about 150 years," admitted Mississippi Republican Trent Lott, the committee's former chair. There are two ways senators can obtain desirable items: one, they get the furniture, paintings, and other things they want declared "surplus" so they can buy them for pennies on the dollar. The other way is more direct—they just steal it. Lott said the intention of the bill is honorable but it might be a moot point. . . . "Most of the stuff is not worth having" because "the good stuff" has already been pilfered.

THE PENTAGON'S MISSILE DEFENSE AGENCY (MDA) CLAIMED THAT ITS JUNE 2003 TEST LAUNCH OF AN SM-3 ROCKET IN HAWAII WAS A ROARING SUCCESS—EVEN THOUGH IT FAILED TO HIT THE INCOMING MISSILE IT WAS PROGRAMMED TO SHOOT DOWN. EXPLAINING THIS CONFUSING CONCLUSION, MDA SPOKESMAN CHRIS TAYLOR SAID, "[I]NTERCEPT WAS NOT THE PRIMARY OBJECTIVE," BUT RATHER IT WAS THE GATHERING OF "GREAT ENGINEERING DATA."

HIS TALKING AIN'T GOT
MORE BETTER

"**I** want it to be said that the Bush administration was a results-oriented administration, because I believe the results of focusing our attention and energy on teaching children to read and having an education system that's responsive to the child and to the parents, as opposed to mired in a system that refuses to change, will make America what we want it to be, a literate country and a hopefuller country."
—*George W. Bush, Washington, D.C., January 11, 2001*

Reading quotes like this just makes me feel joyfuller.

"I glance at the headlines just to kind of get a flavor for what's moving. I rarely read the stories, and get briefed by people who are probably read the news themselves."
—*George W. Bush, Washington, D.C., September 21, 2003*

CRUEL AND UNUSUAL PUNISHMENT

In 2002, a lawsuit demanding nearly $1 billion in compensation (from Saddam Hussein's frozen assets) was filed by seventeen U.S. pilots who were captured and beaten by Saddam forces in the 1991 Gulf War. A federal judge ruled in their favor in 2003, but an appeals court tossed out the case, citing a 2003 postinvasion law requested by the Bush administration to authorize use of the frozen assets to help rebuild Iraq. To add to the torture that these servicemen have already suffered, Defense Secretary Donald Rumsfeld has publicly conceded that the Iraqi detainees who were abused in 2003 at the Abu Ghraib prison should be compensated. The cruel irony is that in 1991 the American servicemen suffered far greater torture and abuse than being led around on a dog leash.

"One of my hardest parts of my job is to console the family members who have lost their life."
—*George W. Bush, Prime Time Press Conference, Washington D.C., April 13, 2004*

LABOR PAINS

In early January 2001, President George W. Bush nominated Linda Chavez to be in his Cabinet as Secretary of Labor. The newly elected President was excited about one of his first Cabinet nominations. So excited he had trouble finding the right words.

"I would have to ask the questioner. I haven't had a chance to ask the questioners the question they've been questioning. On the other hand, I firmly believe she'll be a fine Secretary of Labor. And I've got confidence in Linda Chavez. She is a—she'll bring an interesting perspective to the Labor Department."
—*George W. Bush, Austin, Texas, January 8, 2001*

"I do remain confident in Linda. She'll make a fine labor secretary. From what I've read in the press accounts, she's perfectly qualified."
—*George W. Bush, Austin, Texas, January 8, 2001*

I'm sure Bush was surprised when he read later press accounts; Linda Chavez removed her name as nominee for Secretary of Labor after it was discovered she was employing an illegal alien as a live-in house worker.

EXACTLY SIX MONTHS AFTER SEPTEMBER 11, 2001, THE IMMIGRATION AND NATURALIZATION SERVICES (INS) APPROVED STUDENT-VISA APPLICATIONS FOR MARWAN ALSHEHHI AND MOHAMED ATTA, TWO OF THE HIJACKERS WHO FLEW JETLINERS INTO THE WORLD TRADE CENTER.

OVERLOOKED OVERTIME

You think your boss is stingy when it comes to overtime pay? Well, a federal judge in Washington, D.C., ruled in November 2002 that for approximately twenty years, the U.S. Department of Justice (that's right, the Department of Justice) has flagrantly refused to pay attorneys overtime, which is a violation of federal law. Court of Claims Judge Robert H. Hodges, Jr., said the department apparently just decided to declare itself exempt from the overtime-pay law for attorneys and had been keeping two sets of time sheets (or "two sets of books"): one for pay, one to track time on cases.

I wonder if the U.S. Department of Justice lawyers can sue the U.S. Department of Justice and count the work they do toward their paycheck? (If they can . . . you know they will.)

"I mentioned early on that I recognize there are hurdles, and we're going to achieve those hurdles."
—*George W. Bush, Washington, D.C., January 22, 2003*

AS I GAZE INTO MY CRYSTAL BALL ...

"**T**he only other comment I'd make is that everyone who reads the papers today knows that one of the issues that the world is really thinking about and talking about and wondering about is this issue of preemption, the issue of preventive action. I would use the phrase anticipatory self-defense. Because if a terrorist can attack at any time at any place using any technique, and you know it's physically impossible to defend at every place at every time against every conceivable technique, then you know the only way you can have to defend yourself is to anticipate that attack and preemptively do something about it."

—*Secretary of Defense Donald Rumsfeld, interview with the National Journalists Roundtable, August 5, 2002*

Basically, "anticipatory self-defense means" attack first and ask questions later.

———◆———

"I would be happy to respond to questions assuming that they're civil, amusing, and penetrating. [Laughter] I notice all the hands are going down."

—*Secretary of Defense Donald Rumsfeld, Fort Leonard Wood, Missouri, September 14, 2004*

TURKEY AND STUFFING

Believe it or not there is an organization called the National Wild Turkey Federation (NWTF) in Edgefield, South Carolina. According to the United States Department of Agriculture, the NWTF "supports public conservation education, especially that concerning wild turkey hunting as a traditional North American sport." And who helps support these wild turkey hunting conservation educators? We do. The NWTF gobbled up $469,000 in federal grants in 2005 and $238,000 in 2004. So while these fellows saunter through the woods in their camouflage suits and their shotguns on the hunt for wild turkeys—we taxpayers are getting royally plucked.

"The ambassador and the general were briefing me on the——the vast majority of Iraqis want to live in a peaceful, free world. And we will find these people and we will bring them to justice."
—*George W. Bush, Washington, D.C., October 27, 2003*

A PITCH TO THE OUTSIDE

BUSH: It was my way to—to help kick off the baseball season.
SPORTSCASTER: That's neat.
BUSH: I, I really think it's, uhh—an integral part of the—fabric of
our society, and, uhh—I'm, I'm gonna try to do my part to
make sure baseball gets the notoriety it deserves.

—St. Louis, Missouri, April 5, 2004

With attacking cameramen and average salaries of $2.6 million,
baseball doesn't need any more notoriety.

"We honor the servicemen and women of Great Britain,
Bulgaria, Denmark, El Salvador, Estonia, Hungary,
Italy, Latvia, the Netherlands, Poland, Slovakia, Spain,
Thailand, and Ukraine have died."
—George W. Bush, Washington, D.C., September 23, 2004

I'M NOT AN ANIMAL ... I'M A HUMAN BEING!

In January 2003, the U.S. Court of International Trade made a landmark ruling on the federal Tariff Codes—a ruling that still vibrates through the very fabric of our society. They declared the Marvel Comics X-Men characters to be "nonhuman creatures"—oh, the humanity! From geeks, dorks, and dweebs around the world came a wailing and a gnashing of teeth—everyone knows the characters are mutant humans. But it was actually a Marvel Comics affiliate who called them nonhuman and for a very human reason: money. At the time of the dispute, U.S. Customs taxed "human" re-creations (called "dolls") at 12 percent while imports of nonhuman re-creations (called "toys") were taxed at 6.8 percent. Suddenly, Marvel's tax burden changed from 12 percent to 6.8— changed just like Mystique.

"There's what they call 'actionable intelligence,' to which our military has responded on a quick basis is improving."
—*George W. Bush, Washington, D.C., December 15, 2003*

A PARTY OF ONE

ARI FLEISCHER: "And the President's hope is that other Democrats will follow the lead of those Democrats who have chosen to vote with the Republicans and with the President. He praises those Democrats who are voting in a bipartisan fashion tomorrow, he thinks they're doing the right thing for the country. He hopes that their example will lead others to do the same."

Actual number of Democrats who voted for the "bipartisan" bill—1.

"If an insurance carrier can spread risk across a variety of people or a variety of firms, it makes it more likely his health care goes down."
—*George W. Bush, Washington, D.C., March 16, 2004*

HOPEFULLY HE MEANT "HIS HEALTH CARE COSTS GOES DOWN" BUT YOU NEVER KNOW.

JUST RELAX AND OPEN YOUR WALLET

Among the programs approved during the Clinton administration but immediately axed when Bush took office was an $860,000 initiative to teach self-esteem to public housing tenants. The program was developed by a career Housing and Urban Development official who was a priest of the International Metaphysical Ministry (I'm not joking). The priest, who was also the program's chief trainer, employed the use of colors, meditation, aromatherapy, and "applied kinesiology." The priest said she was "shocked" that something so successful was eliminated.

"Now, there's some rules, and it's important for you to know the rules. One, you can't take your money that you set aside in the personal account and go to the racetrack.... Secondly, you can't pull it all out when it comes time to your— you can't take it all and then go to the track."
—*George W. Bush, Tampa, Florida, February 4, 2005*

IS IT JUST ME OR DO THE FIRST RULE AND THE SECOND RULE SOUND THE SAME?

ASK ME NO QUESTIONS
AND I'LL TELL YOU NO LIES

Russell Mokhiber, editor of the Washington, D.C.–based *Corporate Crime Reporter,* had the uncanny ability to shake the always-in-control Press Secretary, Ari Fleisher.

RUSS MOKHIBER: Ari, two questions. Why is the President appointing convicted criminals like Elliot Abrams to policy positions in the White House?

ARI FLEISCHER: Russell, you asked that question last week.

RUSS MOKHIBER: I did not ask that question last week.

ARI FLEISCHER: You asked it about somebody else. I dispute the premise of your question.

RUSS MOKHIBER: I have a second question.

ARI FLEISCHER: I dispute the premise of your second question.

—*Ari Fleisher, then White House press secretary, and Russell Mokhiber, Press Briefing, Washington, D.C., December 9, 2002*

Mr. Mokhiber now works his magic on the current press secretary, Scott McClellan.

> "You cannot lead this world and our country to a better
> tomorrow unless you see a better—
> if you have a vision of a better tomorrow."
> —*George W. Bush, Washington, D.C., November 4, 2004*

ALMOST CORRECTED HIMSELF CORRECTLY—BUT NOT QUITE.

THIS IS A TEST—THIS IS ONLY A TEST

Airport security is a crucial element in the war on terror, right? So it goes without saying that the people in charge of checking luggage for weapons, explosives, and the like, are highly trained, top-notch screeners. Well, in October 2003, the U.S. Transportation Security Administration's inspector general released questions from the final exam for airport screeners. The grueling test was made up of questions like: "How do threats get on board an aircraft?" A. In carry-on bags; B. In checked-in bags; C. In another person's bag; D. All of the above." I know it's harsh to put someone in charge of your safety through such a rigorous exam, but take heart, twenty-two of the exam's twenty-five questions were repeats from previous exams. I wonder if they got extra credit for getting their names right?

"Look, I don't care about the numbers. I know the facts."
—*George W. Bush, St. Petersburg, Florida, March 8, 2002*

RESPONDING TO ECONOMISTS' DELIBERATION ON THE REACTION OF THE AMERICAN ECONOMY TO THE ATTACKS OF SEPTEMBER 11, 2001.

EVEN MORE RANDOM BUSH

"**T**o the American people, 'Marine' is shorthand for 'can do.'"
—*George W. Bush, Washington, D.C., April 22, 2005*

Not actually shorthand seeing as "can do" is shorter than "Marine."

"**T**oday I am pleased to announce that I have nominated an out-standing military officer, Admiral Ed—Ammiral Ed Giambasteen—Deh—Giam—Giambastiani."
—*George W. Bush, Washington, D.C., April 22, 2005*

Stumbling over Admiral Edmund P. Giambastiani, Jr.'s name as his nominee for vice chairman of the Joint Chiefs of Staff.

"**F**or diplomacy to be effective, words must be credible, and no one can now doubt the word of America."
—*George W. Bush, State of the Union Address, January 20, 2004*

"**N**o child should be left behind in the state of South Dakota."
—*George W. Bush, Sioux Falls, South Dakota, November 3, 2002*

IN THE FISCAL YEAR 2005 FEDERAL BUDGET:
$100,000 FOR THE TIGER WOODS FOUNDATION
FOR AT-RISK YOUTH PROGRAMS IN
LOS ALAMITOS, CALIFORNIA.
TIGER HAS NET ASSETS OF NEARLY $32.6 MILLION.

WELCOME BACK TO THE WILD WEST

U.S. Attorney General John Ashcroft took it upon himself to declare that the Second Amendment did not exclusively apply to a "well regulated militia," as the Justice Department had previously understood it. The Second Amendment, whose meaning has been the subject of ongoing debate, reads: "A well regulated militia, being necessary to the security of a free state, the right of the people to keep and bear arms, shall not be infringed," now gives fundamental gun-toting rights to individuals according to one interpretation. It's a crappy sentence and had the founders used better punctuation, started a new sentence, or clarified their original intent we wouldn't have a problem. Thanks to Mr. Ashcroft's version, a group of eleven alleged members of San Francisco's Big Block street gang claimed in a court filing in June 2002 that they have a constitutional right to carry guns. That's right, if the people have the right to keep and bear arms that means all the people have a right to keep and bear arms—even criminals.

U.S. ATTORNEY GENERAL JOHN ASHCROFT LOST HIS U.S. SENATE REELECTION RACE ON NOVEMBER 8, 2000, TO MISSOURI GOVERNOR MEL CARNAHAN—WHO WAS DEAD. CARNAHAN DIED DURING THE CAMPAIGN BUT HIS WIFE RAN IN HIS PLACE AND STILL COLLECTED ENOUGH VOTES TO BEAT ASHCROFT. HE WAS THEN NOMINATED BY GEORGE W. BUSH TO BE HIS ATTORNEY GENERAL.

LUMBERING THROUGH THE DEBATE

JOHN KERRY: The president got $84 from a timber company
that he owns, and he's counted as a small business. Dick
Cheney's counted as a small business. That's how they do
things. That's just not right.

BUSH: I own a timber company? [Laughter] That's news to me.
[Laughter] Need some wood?

—*Second Presidential Debate, St. Louis, Missouri, October 8, 2004*

Actually, according to his own 2003 financial disclosure form,
Bush does own part interest in LSTF, LLC, a limited-liability
company organized "for the purpose of the production of trees
for commercial sales." You can read the details at factcheck.org
(the Web site Dick Cheney got wrong during the VP debate).

THE FEDERAL COMMUNICATIONS COMMISSION
RULED IN OCTOBER 2003 THAT THE WORD
"F***ING" SPOKEN BY U2 SINGER BONO DURING
THE LIVE TELECAST OF THE GOLDEN GLOBES
WAS NOT OBSCENE LANGUAGE. THE FCC
REMARKED THE WORD WAS NOT USED IN A SEXU-
AL CONTEXT BUT RATHER TO EMPHASIZE THE
WORD "BRILLIANT."

WOULD YOU LIKE TO PLAY A GAME?

In December 2001, the Pentagon, citing intelligence sources, revealed that thousands of Sony PlayStation 2s may have been purchased by Iraqi sources (possibly to play the computer version of "Where in the World Is Osama bin Laden?"). Officials fear that the Iraqis could capitalize on the device's powerful computer processor and video cards and incorporate them into weapons systems. A Sony spokesman didn't deny this potential use of the PlayStation 2, but he did say it was unlikely anyone could buy thousands of units.

I agree—do you know how long I had to stand in line to buy just one?

"Recession means that people's incomes, at the employer level, are going down, basically, relative to costs, people are getting laid off."
—*George W. Bush, Washington, D.C., February 19, 2004*

ALL YOU NEED IS LOVE

"**M**issy Johnson's a fantastic young lady I met in Charlotte, North Carolina, she and her son, Bryan. They came to see me. Her husband, P.J., got killed. He'd been in Afghanistan, went to Iraq. You know, it's hard work to try to love her as best as I can, knowing full well that the decision I made caused her——her loved one to be in harm's way."

——George W. Bush, First Presidential Debate,
Coral Gables, Florida, September 30, 2004

"You need to have you a governor in the great state of Mississippi who understands what it means to create an environment for job growth, who hurts when he hears people are working, and that man is Haley Barbour."

——George W. Bush, Gulfport, Mississippi, November 1, 2003

P.S.: TO ADD INSULT TO INJURY, BESIDES BUSH'S SLIP OF THE TONGUE, THE WHITE HOUSE WEB SITE SPELLED HALEY BARBOUR'S NAME INCORRECTLY.

BETCHA CAN'T EAT JUST ONE

I'm sure we've all heard the expression, "He's so dumb he can't walk and chew gum at the same time," right? But in January 2002, President Bush changed that phrase to include "pretzels" and "watch football." While the President was at the White House watching the Baltimore-Miami NFL playoff game he got a pretzel lodged in his throat and passed out. "I hit the deck," is how Bush described his snack-attack. The President got a scrape and a large bruise on his left cheekbone, plus a bruise on his lower lip (and a bruise on his ego, I'm sure). "If my mother is listening, Mother, I should have listened to you: 'Always chew your pretzels before you swallow,'" Bush said jokingly.

The CIA moved Mr. Salty to the top of its most-wanted list.

IN THE FISCAL YEAR 2005 FEDERAL BUDGET: $6,285,000 FOR WOOD UTILIZATION RESEARCH (ALASKA, IDAHO, MAINE, MICHIGAN, MINNESOTA, MISSISSIPPI, NORTH CAROLINA, OREGON, TENNESSEE, WASHINGTON, AND WEST VIRGINIA). SINCE 1985, $79 MILLION HAS BEEN ROOTED OUT OF THE TAXPAYERS FOR THIS RESEARCH.

IT'S IN HIS GENES

"That's an interesting question because in the last week or so there have been several articles saying that I'm impatient or unhappy with the pace of things, and the truth is the men and women in the military are doing a terrific job. . . . On the other hand, I can understand why the stories come out because I am, I suppose, genetically impatient."

—*Secretary of Defense Donald Rumsfeld, interview with the National Journalists Roundtable, August 5, 2002*

HE WHO SMELT IT, DEALT IT

Military researchers revealed in July 2001 that they were working on a new weapon—not a weapon of mass destruction, but a weapon of mass disgustion. They are attempting to develop the ultimate stink bomb. Scientists sniffed their way through some of the most disgusting smells in the world and announced their winners—excrement and rotting foods and carcasses. But these are not just any piles of excrement and rotting carcasses; they have been "improved" and enhanced to even fouler levels. When these two substances are mixed, they will produce an odor so putrid it will not only immediately disperse crowds but also stimulate the brain tissue, provoking the feeling of fear that other unrecognizable stimuli do.

I think a guy I was standing behind in a recent checkout line was a test subject.

"I promise you I will listen to what has been said here, even though I wasn't here."
—*George W. Bush, Waco, Texas, August 13, 2002*

FABULOUS, SIMPLY FABULOUS

"**A**nd we'll prevail, because we're a fabulous nation, and we're a fabulous nation because we're a nation full of fabulous people."
    —*George W. Bush, Atlanta, Georgia, January 31, 2002*

"**A**nd that thing greater than ourselves is freedom. And that thing greater than ourselves is a country based upon fabulous values."
    —*George W. Bush, Cedar Rapids, Iowa, April 15, 2002*

"**T**his is a fabulous country in which we live, it is. And it's because the people are fabulous."
    —*George W. Bush, Washington, D.C., June 4, 2002*

"We want to make sure our wallets all across the country are healthy."
    —*George W. Bush, Philadelphia, Pennsylvania,*
    January 31, 2004

STOP YOUR WINE-ING

In 1920, Congress passed the Eighteenth Amendment to the Constitution, called the Prohibition of Intoxicating Liquors, and from 1920 to 1933 it was illegal to make, buy, sell, import, or export booze. Now the government sponsors and even subsidizes makers of alcohol, specifically winemakers. In Fiscal Year 2005, $1,850,000 was given for the viticulture consortium (California, New York, and Pennsylvania). Cornell University was the recipient of the grant, and according to their Web site, "this grant is to maintain a consortium through which research in support of viticulture and the viticulture industry will be coordinated. . . ." Wine sales in the United States grew to a record 627 million gallons in 2003, with a retail value of $21.6 billion. California wineries produced 417 million gallons, which was 67 percent (by volume) of the market, or two of every three bottles sold in the United States. I'm sure the wine industry raised a toast to Congress while you and I got corked.

"People sometimes say what's more important than the country is my politics."
—*George W. Bush, Washington, D.C., January 3, 2005*

CROSSED WIRES ON *CROSSFIRE*

PAUL BEGALA, *CROSSFIRE* HOST: President Bush took to the podium of the White House briefing room today but spent much of the press conference on the defensive. He was peppered with questions about his role, if any, in controversial accounting practices and insider stock sales when he was a director of the Harken Energy Company.

(BEGIN VIDEO CLIP)

GEORGE W. BUSH, PRESIDENT OF THE UNITED STATES: No malfeance, no attempt to hide anything. It was just an accounting firm making a decision, along with the corporate officers, as to how to account for a complex transition.

(END VIDEO CLIP)

BEGALA: No one in the White House press corps there asked the president what malfeance or transitions were. . . .

"There you are. You look just like yourself."
—*George W. Bush, Washington, D.C., February 24, 2003*

SAID UPON SEEING FORMER OSU QUARTERBACK AND
ESPN ANALYST KIRK HERBSTREIT IN PERSON.

A REAL SENSE OF SECURITY

To the Department of Homeland Security, it's no laughing matter, but Ernest Istook (R-Oklahoma), a member of the House Homeland Security Committee, accused the department of making "a joke" out of President Bush's 2003 order to compile a comprehensive list of possible terrorist targets in the United States. Others joined the outraged congressman in December 2004 to express their concern over the still incomplete list. As of that date the list contained eighty thousand potential domestic terror targets including such inexplicable sites as miniature golf courses and water parks. But according to Robert Liscouski, head of infrastructure protection at the Homeland Security Department, it isn't the department's fault. It receives its information, he said, from state and local government and private industry in identifying sites.

Why are the local governments having so much trouble? Well, according to a July 2004 memo from former Homeland Security Secretary Tom Ridge, local officials "lack clear guidelines and standards" from his department to help them determine which sites to include. "Absent such clear delineation, it is impossible to justify any item contained on the national list," Ridge wrote. Liscouski, still in spin mode, said officials have started analyzing the information. "We have a good handle on what the top targets in the United States are," he said. "It's not going fast, but it's coming along."

Wow, I feel safer already, don't you?

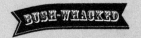
"Laura reminded me, in July of 2002,
on the television screens came
to the notation,
'America is Marching to War.'"
—*George W. Bush, Louisville, Kentucky,*
February 26, 2004

BUSH BY A NOSE

"**I** remember campaigning in Chicago one time, and the guy said, would you ever deficit spend? I said, 'Well, only if we were at war, or the country was in recession, or there was a national emergency.' I didn't realize we were going to get the trifecta."
—*George W. Bush, Philadelphia, Pennsylvania, April 3, 2002*

Only Bush could compaire three tragic events to a horse race.

IN THE FISCAL YEAR 2005 FEDERAL BUDGET: $150,000 FOR TURFGRASS RESEARCH IN BEAVER, WEST VIRGINIA.

HURLING INTO SPACE

In October 2004, NASA announced it was retiring the KC-135 plane, nicknamed the "Weightless Wonder" and the "Vomit Comet," which had long been used to train astronauts for weightlessness in flight. A NASA official told reporters that the aircrews had kept a running total of the amount of astronaut vomit cleaned up over the years and that the total was at least 285 gallons.

Makes one wonder how much of that space spew was Tang.

"It reads like a mystery, a novel. It's well written."
—*George W. Bush, Crawford, Texas, July 26, 2004*

BUSH WAS REMARKING ON THE 9/11 COMMISSION'S REPORT.

MAKE HAY WHILE THE SUN SHINES

"I understand how risky agriculture can be. It wouldn't be so risky if we could control the weather. That's one of the things we haven't figured out how to do yet. It wouldn't be so risky if we could make it rain all the time. There would be hay to feed the cows. Somehow, that doesn't happen all the time. I know."

—*George W. Bush, Denver, Colorado, February 8, 2002*

"People tell me that Senator Edwards got picked for his good looks, his sex appeal, and his great hair. I say to them—how do you think I got the job?"

—*Dick Cheney, Republican National Convention, New York City, September 1, 2004*

THE GOVERNMENT COOK BOOK

When the auditors at the Defense Contract Audit Agency in New York City learned well in advance that a number of files would be checked by a review team, they leaped into action. It took them 1,139 hours, the equivalent of more than forty-seven days, to get everything in good order for the review—they wanted everything just right. According to a report by the inspector general's office, they were busy altering, fabricating, falsifying, and otherwise doctoring the records. The task of rewriting the files was so daunting that auditors were brought in from other offices to help make the changes (costing taxpayers more than $1,600 in travel expenses). These fabrications of the defense agency, which audits government contracts looking for waste and fraud, were discovered in 2001, but the report was not made public until January 6, 2004. From now on review teams will only give forty-eight hours advance notice as to the files they wish to inspect. Fabricating records is nothing new to the inspector general's office—in fact, in 2001, they were discovered destroying documents and replacing them with fakes themselves.

"She is a fabulous First Lady. I was a lucky man when she said, yes, I agree to marry you. I love her dearly, and I'm proud of the job she's doing on behalf of all Americans. Just like I love my brother."
—*George W. Bush, Jacksonville, Florida, September 9, 2003*

OKAY, I'M VERY UNCOMFORTABLE WITH THIS STATEMENT.

A LEADING LEADER

"It's an interesting question about leadership. Does a leader lead, or does a leader follow? Does a leader lead opinion, or does a leader try to chase public opinion? My view is the leader leads. . . . I understand a leader can't do everything. And so, therefore, a leader must be willing to surround himself, in my case, with smart, capable, honorable people. A leader must be willing to listen. And then a leader must be decisive enough to make a decision and stick by it. In politics, in order to lead, you've got to know what you believe. You have to stand on principle; you have to believe in certain values. And you must defend them at all costs. A politician who takes a poll to figure out what to believe is a politician who is constantly going to be trying to lead through—it's like a dog chasing its tail. And, finally, any leader must—in order to lead, must understand—must have a vision about where you're going."

—*George W. Bush, Petersburg University,*
St. Petersburg, Russia, May 25, 2002

Leading a lecture on leaders and leading to a leading university.

THE UNITED STATES HAS BEEN KICKED OFF THE
INTERNATIONAL NARCOTICS CONTROL BOARD,
THE U.N.'S DRUG CONTROL AGENCY, AND THE U.N.
HUMAN RIGHTS COMMISSION. BOTH VOTES WERE
BY SECRET BALLOT OF OTHER COUNTRIES.

WHAT'S IN A NAME?

One issue that was never addressed during the presidential debates between George W. Bush and John Kerry is that John Kerry is a "horny jerk." That phrase didn't come from some Republican hatchetman, it came from anagramgenius.com—because if you jumble the letters of John Kerry's name you get "horny jerk." Other politicians didn't fare so well either. For example, anagrams for George W. Bush include, "He grew bogus," and "Ugh! Sewer bog." Just George Bush becomes "Be Ogre Hugs" and the amazingly accurate, "Beer Hugs Go." The letters in Dick Cheney turn into "Check De Yin" or his alter ego "Cindy Cheek." If you input "Vice President Dick Cheney" you get, "Prick's ethic: Deny Evidence."

*T*he *Da Vinci Code*'s got nothing on this one.

"They can get in line like those who have been here legally and have been working to become a citizenship in a legal manner."
—*George W. Bush, discussing immigrant workers, Washington, D.C., December 20, 2004*

NOT THE CRAW—THE CRAW!

DONALD RUMSFELD: No. I mean, this is an unusual situation. People are looking for us—you know, it's the old glass box at the—at the gas station, where you're using those little things trying to pick up the prize, and you can't find it. [Laughter] It's—and it's all these arms are going down in there, and so you keep dropping it and picking it up again and moving it, but—some of you are probably too young to remember those —those glass boxes, but—[Laughter]—they used to have them at all the gas stations when I was a kid. [Laughter]

—*Secretary of Defense Donald Rumsfeld, DOD Press Briefing, December 6, 2001*

Rumsfeld was explaining how the United States, with its limited number of deployed troops, could detain soldiers and leaders of al Qaeda or the Taliban who choose to surrender.

"The truth of the matter is, if you listen carefully, Saddam would still be in power if he [John Kerry] were the President of the United States, and the world would be a lot better off."

—*George W. Bush, Second Presidential Debate, St. Louis, Missouri, October 8, 2004*

SAYING THE EXACT OPPOSITE OF WHAT HE MEANT TO SAY (OF COURSE, WITH BUSH ONE NEVER KNOWS FOR SURE).

PUT A LID ON IT

President Bush's advance team has struck again. It was noted earlier in this book that the advance team had been responsible for getting the MISSION ACCOMPLISHED banner aboard the USS *Abraham Lincoln* for Bush's spontaneous delivery by jet, and now they've put their stamp on another event. When President Bush addressed a group of local officials and small-business owners at the JB Logistics shipping company in St. Louis, on January 21, 2003, he stood in front of a huge pile of boxes with MADE IN U.S.A. stamped on them. Not only were there boxes behind the President, they were also in front of him and to the side—all with the MADE IN U.S.A. stamp clearly visible. The only thing is that the boxes originally said MADE IN CHINA, as they contained items that were made in China, but the Bush team painstakingly covered over those labels with ones of their own making.

Another in a long line of Bush cover-ups.

"From its birth in the 1630s, the Guard protected the early colonists and helped win the War on Independence."
—*George W. Bush, Las Vegas, Nevada, September 14, 2004*

A STATE OF CONFUSION

Welsh-born singing phenomenon Charlotte Church was fifteen years old when she met President George W. Bush in October 2001. According to Church she was flustered when "He [Bush] said, 'So what state is Wales in?' I said, 'Erm, it's a separate country next to England,' and he went, 'Oh, okay.' I didn't know what to say."

—MSNBC, October 30, 2001

Don't worry, Charlotte, we don't know what to say about him most of the time, either.

"I don't think my opponent has got the right view about the world to make us safe. I really don't. First of all, I don't think he can succeed in Iraq. And if Iraq were to fail, it'd be a haven for terrorists, and there would be money and the world would be much more dangerous."

—George W. Bush, Second Presidential Debate, St. Louis, Missouri, October 8, 2004

CAN SOMEONE EXPLAIN THE "THERE WOULD BE MONEY" LINE?

WHERE'S THE SENS IN THAT?

As our country watched the orange terrorism alert flash on the television screen, Attorney General John Ashcroft was busy smoking out the real enemy—bong makers. Ashcroft's crack team from the Drug Enforcement Administration (DEA) fired up Operation Pipe Dream and Operation Headhunter, as Ashcroft named the raids, and arrested fifty-five people and confiscated "tons and tons" of drug paraphernalia (not drugs, not drug dealers, but pipes, bongs, roach clips, and the like). The majority of the February 2003 arrests were head shop owners and owners of Internet sites that sold paraphernalia, but the biggest villain to be weeded out was Tommy Chong of Chong Glass (formerly of the comedy team Cheech and Chong). Chong was sentenced to nine months in prison and paid a $20,000 fine.

I hope putting this notorious criminal in jail didn't backlog all the trials, arrests, and incarcerations of the terrorists responsible for the attacks of 9/11—oh, that's right, there haven't been any.

***

"No child in America should be left behind in this country."
—*George W. Bush, St. Louis, Missouri, January 22, 2003*

HERE'S THE CHURCH, HERE'S THE STEEPLE, OPEN THE DOOR...

"It's an important concept for our fellow citizens to understand, that no one in need will ever be forced to choose a faith-based provider. That's an important concept for people to understand. What that means is if you're the Methodist church and you sponsor an alcohol treatment center, they can't say only Methodists, only Methodists who drink too much can come to our program. 'All Drunks Are Welcome' is what the sign ought to say."

—*George W. Bush, Washington, D.C., March 1, 2005*

Army Lieutenant General Lt. Gen. William G. "Jerry" Boykin, Deputy Undersecretary of Defense for Intelligence, said of a Muslim militia leader in Somalia: "Well, you know what I knew, that my God was bigger than his. I knew that my God was a real God, and his was an idol."

—Los Angeles Times, *October 16, 2003*

SHRIMPING IN A SEA OF GREEN

In 2005, Congress earmarked $3,973,000 for shrimp aquaculture research (Arizona, Hawaii, Louisiana, Massachusetts, Mississippi, South Carolina, and Texas). This money is used to help the shrimp industry find ways to increase productivity, fight disease, and other shrimp activities. Since 1985, $61 million has been netted for this research: that's a lot of pork for shrimp. So is the shrimp industry short on cash? No way. Currently, shrimp is the number-one selling seafood consumed in the United States. Americans eat more than 1 billion pounds of shrimp each year and the worldwide demand is expected to grow; shrimp already generates a retail trade of $6 billion per year. Why does Congress constantly subsidize private industry and big business? Pork programs bring work and money to local communities and that, in turn, means votes for the politician who stewarded the programs. And big business contributes heavily to political candidates who keep them on the government dole.

"[T]he illiteracy level of our children are appalling."
—*George W. Bush, Washington, D.C., January 23, 2004*

I'VE GOT MY SIGHTS SET ON YOU

"The situation is this: We are going to address fixed targets as we find them. We are going to address emerging targets as we find them. Things will not be necessarily continuous. The fact that they are something other than perfectly continuous ought not to be characterized as a pause. There will be some things that people will see. There will be some things that people won't see. And life goes on."

—*Secretary of Defense Donald Rumsfeld,*
DOD Press Briefing, October 12, 2001

"I have—I understand everybody in this country doesn't agree with the decisions I've made. And I made some tough decisions. But people know where I stand."

—*George W. Bush, First Presidential Debate,*
Coral Gables, Florida, September 30, 2004

HE EITHER MADE A MISTAKE IN HIS SPEECH OR HE'S BEEN HIDING THIS FACT FROM ONE HALF THE PEOPLE IN THE UNITED STATES.

THE POT CALLING THE KETTLE...

In October 2003, Barbara Bush (George's mother) described the Democratic candidates for President as a "sorry group." The candidates included a decorated war veteran (John Kerry), a Rhodes Scholar and top West Point grad (four-star general Wesley Clark), Senator Joseph Lieberman, Senator John Edwards, former Governor Howard Dean, Senator Carol Mosley Braun, Senator Bob Graham, the Reverend Al Sharpton, former House Minority Leader Dick Gephardt, and four-term Congressman Dennis Kucinich, and numerous other public servants. Barbara's group includes two granddaughters arrested for underage drinking (Jenna and Barbara), another granddaughter with two drug-related arrests (Noelle), a son (George) arrested for drunk driving (twice), another son (Neil) who's an admitted whoremonger, and another son (Jeb) investigated for HMO abuse. So who's sorry now?

"But we've got a big border in Texas, with Mexico obviously—and we've got a big border with Canada—Arizona is affected."
—George W. Bush, Washington, D.C., June 24, 2004

I NEED TO LOOK AT MY MAP AGAIN BECAUSE EITHER ARIZONA HAS SHIFTED NORTH OR CANADA HAS INVADED.

REALLY, I'M BUSHED

WASHINGTON POST: Will you talk to Senate Democrats about your privatization plan?

BUSH: You mean, the personal savings accounts?

WASHINGTON POST: Yes, exactly. Scott has been—

BUSH: We don't want to be editorializing, at least in the questions.

WASHINGTON POST: You used partial privatization yourself last year, sir.

BUSH: Yes?

WASHINGTON POST: Yes, three times in one sentence. We had to figure this out, because we're in an argument with the RNC [Republican National Committee] about how we should actually word this. [Post staff writer] Mike Allen, the industrious Mike Allen, found it.

BUSH: Allen did what now?

WASHINGTON POST: You used partial privatization.

BUSH: I did, personally?

WASHINGTON POST: Right.

BUSH: When?

WASHINGTON POST: To describe it.

BUSH: When, when was it?

WASHINGTON POST: Mike said it was right around the election.

BUSH: Seriously?

WASHINGTON POST: It was right around the election. We'll send it over.

BUSH: I'm surprised. Maybe I did. It's amazing what happens when you're tired.

—*Aboard* Air Force One, *January 14, 2005*

It might serve Bush well if he just claims he was exhausted and didn't really mean to declare war on Iraq.

IN A CLASSIC CASE OF CATCH-22, THE AMERICAN CIVIL LIBERTIES UNION FILED A LAWSUIT IN APRIL 2004, CLAIMING PART OF THE PATRIOT ACT (A PUBLIC DOCUMENT) WAS UNCONSTITU- TIONAL. BUT WITHOUT JUSTICE DEPARTMENT PERMISSION THEY COULDN'T MAKE PUBLIC THE LAWSUIT'S CLAIM BECAUSE SUCH DISCLOSURE IS FORBIDDEN BY THE PATRIOT ACT.

TOUGH-TALKING TEXAN

In July 2001, on his first visit to Britain as President, George Bush said he was excited to meet the queen for a second time, the first time as President, and during the original meeting, "Mum and Dad invited Laura and me to a private lunch (with the queen) right here in this dining room," gesturing to the private quarters of the White House. "I found her charming, she was great, a wonderful sense of humor. My mother and I, we like to tease, and she fit right in. She was neat." That's probably the first time the queen of England has ever been referred to as "neat," especially by the leader of the most powerful country in the world; makes one feel right proud, don't it?

IN THE FISCAL YEAR 2005 FEDERAL BUDGET: $3 MILLION ADDED BY THE HOUSE FOR A HOUSE STAFF FITNESS FACILITY (EVEN THOUGH THERE ARE TWO PRIVATE GYMS IN PROXIMITY). SINCE CONGRESS CAN'T TRIM THE FAT FROM THE BUDGET THEY'LL AT LEAST BE ABLE TO TRIM THE FAT FROM AROUND THEIR WAISTS— AT THE TAXPAYERS' EXPENSE.

WHERE'S THE AMAZING KRESKIN WHEN YOU NEED HIM?

"**I** also believe that some of the decisions I've made up to now have affected our standing in parts of the world. I remember in the debates, somebody asked me about Europe. And I said, well, they wanted us to join the International Criminal Court, and I chose— I said, that's not the right posture for the United States of America, or some saying I should have negotiated with [Yasser] Arafat for the four years I was President—obviously, prior to his death."

—*George W. Bush, aboard* Air Force One, *January 14, 2005*

I know it's a long, boring paragraph, but it really pays off at the end, doesn't it?

<hr />

"Except for the occasional heart attack, I never felt better."

–*Vice President Dick Cheney, June 2003*

THUNDER DOME

This is going to sound like an idea I made up, but I could never come up with an idea this bizarre: an indoor rainforest. It's a 4.5-acre indoor rainforest project slated to be built in Coralville, Iowa. This boondoggle is the brainchild of Des Moines businessman Ted Townsend, who's had trouble raising the money to start construction (go figure). But now, thanks to Senate Finance Committee Chairman Charles Grassley (R-Iowa) and his $50 million donation to the project (courtesy of us taxpayers), it's closer to reaching its goal of $180 million.

"Tommy is a good listener, and he's a pretty good actor, too. He can get things done. Action man, we call him."

—*George W. Bush, August 13, 2002*

BUSH IS REFERRING TO (NOW FORMER) HEALTH AND HUMAN SERVICES SECRETARY TOMMY THOMPSON.

WE'VE BEEN SISTERS FOR AS LONG AS I CAN REMEMBER

During the Republican National Convention on August 31, 2003, George and Laura Bush's twin daughters, Jenna and Barbara Bush took the stage to introduce their father. Our nation collectively cringed when we heard the comic stylings of the two girls, some of which I've included here:

BARBARA BUSH: We spent the last four years trying to stay out of the spotlight. Sometimes, we did a little better job than others.

[LAUGHTER]

JENNA BUSH: We kept trying to explain to my dad that when we are young and irresponsible, well, we're young and irresponsible.

As they got close to the end of their stand-up routine the audience wasn't sure if the girls were still joking or not.

JENNA BUSH: But contrary to what you might read in the papers, our parents are actually kind of cool. They do know the difference between mono and Bono. When we tell them we're going to see Outkast, they know it's a band and not a bunch of misfits. And if we really beg them, they'll even shake it like a Polaroid picture.

[LAUGHTER]

[APPLAUSE]

BARBARA BUSH: So, okay, maybe they have learned a little pop culture from us, but we've learned a lot more from them about what matters in life, about unconditional love, about focus and discipline.

BARBARA BUSH: They taught us the importance of a good sense of humor, of being open-minded and treating everyone with respect. And we learned the true value of honesty and integrity.

Oh, my gosh, they're so funny. That part about focus and discipline, honesty and integrity nearly split my sides.

"Oh my goodness gracious, what you can buy off the Internet in terms of overhead photography! A trained ape can know an awful lot of what is going on in this world, just by punching on his mouse. For a relatively modest cost!"

—*Secretary of Defense Donald Rumsfeld, June 9, 2001*

ONE POTATO, TWO POTATO,
THREE POTATO, FOUR ...

It's called the International Fund for Ireland and it sounds like a
benefit concert put together by Bono—but unfortunately it isn't.
The International Fund for Ireland (IFI), in support of the Anglo-
Irish Accord, collects funds to be spent for "those projects that hold
the greatest potential for job creation and equal opportunity for the
Irish people." That's Irish people, not Irish-Americans; we're talking about sending your tax dollars to help Irish people living in
Ireland. In the Fiscal Year 2005 Federal Budget, Congress contributed $10 million to the fund. Some of the projects created by
the IFI have included building industrial complexes, a national
water sports center used for coaching top-level athletes, exporting
sweaters, and golf videos. In 2004, Congress contributed
$18,500,000, and in 2003, Congress gave $25 million.

You know giving the fund $439 million since 1986 has really
paid off—I love my new cardigan.

———◆———

"Sometimes it's not easy to be the friend of
George W. Bush —I know that. If you know what I mean."
—*George W. Bush, Houston, Texas, September 12, 2003*

LET ME REPHRASE THAT A DIFFERENT WAY

"**T**he United States has no right, no desire, and no intention to impose our form of government on anyone else. That is one of the main differences between us and our enemies."

—*George W. Bush, 2005 State of the Union address,*
Washington, D.C., February 2, 2005

Later on in the same speech:

"We are in Iraq to achieve a result. A country that is democratic."

— *George W. Bush, 2005 State of the Union address,*
Washington, D.C., February 2, 2005

A U.S. TREASURY DEPARTMENT AUDIT CONDUCTED IN DECEMBER 2002 REVEALED THAT THE INTERNAL REVENUE SERVICE WAS UNABLE TO ACCOUNT FOR 2,300 COMPUTERS SUPPOSEDLY IN ITS EMPLOYEES' HANDS— THAT'S ONE HECK OF A DEDUCTION.

I FEEL SAFER ALREADY

The Homeland Security Fellowship Program offers money to students and university programs interested in pursuing scientific and technological advancements that can be utilized and exploited by the Department of Homeland Security (DHS). In the Fiscal Year 2005 Federal Budget, $40 million was added by Congress to fund this program. In the program's first year of existence (2003), only 101 students participated. Students entering their junior year are awarded full school tuition and fees, a $1,000 monthly stipend for nine months, and $500 weekly for a summer internship (8 to 10 weeks) at a DHS-designated facility. The graduate fellowships include full tuition and fees, a $2,300 monthly stipend for the full year, and the annual awards are renewable for a total of up to three years. Of those 101 students in this terribly costly program, a total of two were hired by DHS. In 2004, a whopping 105 students were enrolled. Since its creation, this program has been awarded $100 million from Congress because this is a great way for members to send pork projects to their home state without question. Who is going to question a program with the words Homeland Security in it?

"We want results in every single classroom
so that one single child is left behind."
—*George W. Bush, Little Rock, Arkansas, November 10, 2003*

MAKES ME WONDER WHAT THAT "ONE SINGLE CHILD"
WHO GOT LEFT BEHIND DID TO DESERVE IT.

DON'T KNOW MUCH ABOUT HISTORY

"**A**fter all, we're at war, and for the first time in our nation's history, part of the battlefront is here at home."
— *George W. Bush, National Association of Manufacturers,*
October 31, 2001

Apparently our President hasn't dipped into the old history books lately. During the War of 1812, while the British were on our soil, they burned down the White House; there were battlefronts all during the Civil War; and during World War II, the Japanese seized the islands of Attu and Kiska (Alaska), bombed Dutch Harbor, Alaska, and shelled Fort Stevens, Oregon, and Santa Barbara, California.

———◆———

IN THE FISCAL YEAR 2005 FEDERAL BUDGET: $75,000 FOR THE PAPER INDUSTRY INTERNATIONAL HALL OF FAME IN APPLETON, WISCONSIN.

IS THIS TRIP REALLY NECESSARY?

The Senate added $10 million in 2005 for intercity bus security grants as part of Homeland Security. The funds were earmarked for "critical security needs" such as driver protection and training, passenger and baggage screening programs, and communications technologies. The Senate doled out this $10 million in case the $10 million they gave out in 2004 wasn't enough. Obviously there was a huge demand and a pressing need for this $20 million in security grants, right? Not exactly. In fact, there was no budget request for the grants in either year—Greyhound Lines, Inc., received unrequested bus security grants on August 27, 2004, totaling $1,603,840. In 2003, their annual revenues totaled a measly $975.5 million. It is estimated that Greyhound has twenty-two million passengers a year and the money yanked out of taxpayer's wallets could have been generated (if needed) by simply adding $.07 to the price of each ticket.

> "I said you were a man of peace.
> I want you to know I took immense crap for that."
> —*George W. Bush, June 3, 2003*

IN CONVERSATION WITH ISRAELI PRIME MINISTER ARIEL SHARON. SOURCE: WASHINGTON POST, "BUSH STICKS TO THE BROAD STROKES."

OUT OF THE BUSH LEAGUE

"**B**ernie Kerik is one of the most accomplished and effective leaders of law enforcement in America. In every position, he has demonstrated a deep commitment to justice, a heart for the innocent, and a record of great success."

—*George W. Bush, on the nomination of Bernard Kerik as Secretary of Homeland Security, December 3, 2004*

Unfortunately, shortly after this glowing recommendation, Bernard Kerik removed his name as nominee when it came to light that he had an illegal alien working at his home. According to the *Washington Post,* "White House officials said they knew in advance about other disclosures now emerging about Kerik's background, including alleged extramarital affairs and reported ties to a construction company with supposed mob connections, but had concluded that they were not disqualifying."

"Let me put it to you bluntly. In a changing world, we want more people to have control over your own life."
—*George W. Bush, Annandale, Virginia, August 9, 2004*

A PUBLIC FINANCIAL CENTER

It's called the Capitol Visitor Center (CVC) and although you might be just a visitor your money is going to stay there forever. In 2005, Congress appropriated $3,270,000 for start-up operations at the CVC. The original projected cost of this center was $265 million, but it's already swollen to an estimated $559 million. The center is designed as a six-level, fifty-five-foot-deep, six-acre addition that will be built under the 202-year-old U.S. Capitol. The center will hold food shops, "two 280-seat theaters, exhibits, gift shops, an auditorium, [and] a new virtual museum." The educational dimension was created so Congress can blow its own grandiose horn; it features how representative government works, tells the "rich" story of Congress, keeps visitors current on the status of congressional activities, and, believe it or not, makes videos of congressional proceedings available for purchase (Zzzzzzzz). So we have the honor of paying over $550 million to see all the great things Congress is doing with our money. I wonder if the gift shop will have T-shirts with "I paid $550 million dollars and all I got was this lousy T-shirt."

"So community colleges are accessible, they're available, they're affordable, and their curriculums don't get stuck. In other words, if there's a need for a certain kind of worker, I presume your curriculums evolved over time."
—*George W. Bush, Niceville, Florida, August 10, 2004*

SLOWLY I TURN,
STEP BY STEP, INCH BY INCH . . .

"**Y**ou see, the evildoers like to hit and then they try to hide. And *slowly, but surely,* we're going to make sure they have no place to hide. *Slowly, but surely,* we're going to move them out of their holes and what they think is safe havens, and get them on the move . . . In my speech to the Congress, I said, sometimes the American people aren't going to see exactly what's taking place on their TV screens. But *slowly, but surely,* the results are coming in . . . We're beginning to share intelligence amongst our nations. We're finding out members of the al Qaeda organization, who they are, where they think they can hide. And we're *slowly, but surely,* bringing them to justice. We're *slowly, but surely,* calling their hand and reining them in."

—*George W. Bush, speaking to employees at the*
Federal Emergency Management Agency (FEMA)
Headquarters, Washington, D.C., October 1, 2001

Since they are government employees the President probably found it necessary to speak slowly, but surely, to them, too.

BUSH-WHACKED

IN THE FISCAL YEAR 2005
FEDERAL BUDGET:
$1 MILLION FOR BROWN TREE SNAKE
RESEARCH. THE BROWN TREE SNAKE
EXISTS ONLY IN GUAM,
IS NOT LIFE THREATENING TO HUMANS,
AND CAN'T SURVIVE IN NORTH AMERICA.
FUNDING THIS RESEARCH IS
QUESTIONABLE AT BEST AND CERTAINLY
HAD NO BUSINESS SLITHERING
ITS WAY INTO THE DEFENSE
APPROPRIATIONS ACT.

I SMELL A RAT

Disney resorts are dream destinations for most families with young children and of course everything is hugely expensive. So how much do you think it will cost you to ride the new Anaheim Resort Transit (ART) bus system that takes you to Disneyland, Disney's California Adventure, and the Anaheim Convention Center, just to name a few destinations? One dollar . . . maybe two dollars? Try three hundred thousand dollars. That's how much taxpayer money has gone into the Anaheim Resort Transit in 2005 thanks to the House of Representatives. The "fleet's dynamic, resort-themed appearance along with its specially trained uniformed drivers heighten the resort district's branding and make it easy for guests to identify the ART product." In 2004, ART received five hundred thousand dollars from the Transportation/Treasury Appropriations bill. Surely the Mouse could cough up enough cheese to pay for a transportation system that takes money-laden tourists to the biggest cash trap in the world or, since it only benefits Anaheim, what if the city of Anaheim paid for their own transportation system?

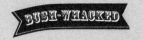

THE OFFICE OF FOREIGN ASSETS
CONTROL, THE DIVISION OF THE U.S.
TREASURY DEPARTMENT THAT IS
RESPONSIBLE FOR UNCOVERING AND
FREEZING THE FINANCIAL ASSETS OF
TERRORISTS, REVEALED IN MAY 2004
THAT IT HAS ONLY FOUR FULL-TIME
AGENTS WORKING THAT TASK. IT HAS
MORE THAN FIVE TIMES THAT MANY
FULL-TIME AGENTS (TWENTY-ONE TO BE
EXACT) INVESTIGATING VIOLATIONS OF
THE ECONOMIC EMBARGO ON CUBA.

THE STRAW POLL THAT BROKE
THE CAMEL'S BACK

After the voting debacle of 2000, our system needed a major upgrade not only in equipment but also in poll workers. Here comes Congress to the rescue. In the 2005 Federal Budget, $200,000 was earmarked for the Help America Vote College Program. The program was proposed by the U.S. Election Assistance Commission to recruit and train poll workers, specifically college students, for the November 2, 2004, presidential election. The program would make sure there were no more hanging chads and that there would be a trained poll worker to help voters properly cast their vote. However, the fiscal 2005 Omnibus Appropriations Act that would supply the funding was passed on November 20, 2004—eighteen days after the November 2 election. Too bad Congress doesn't have an early voting system—then they could screw things up ahead of schedule.

"Of all the people in the world who understand Texas, it's probably Australians."

—*George W. Bush, aboard* Air Force One
en route to Australia, October 22, 2003

MY MIND IS LIKE A SHUT TRAP

"**I**'m a patient man. But I haven't changed my opinion since the last time [King Abdullah of Jordan] was in the Oval Office. And one of the things we will do is consult with our friends. But he just needs to know how I feel. He knows how I feel, I had the opportunity and the honor of explaining that to him before and he'll find out I haven't changed my mind."

—*George W. Bush, Washington, D.C., July 31, 2002*

A not-so-diplomatic way of saying, "If you're thinkin' you can change my mind about something I've made up my mind about like that war in Iraq, then you got another think coming. But, buddy, I can't wait to chew the fat with you."

" So that's——what——there's some ideas. And the—— it's——My job is to, like, think beyond the immediate."
—*George W. Bush, Washington, D.C., April 21, 2004*

DUDE, YOU'RE LIKE, SO AWESOME!

THIS REALLY RATES

The world-famous Biltmore Hotel in Coral Gables, Florida, was the height of luxury in the 1920s—and after its $40 million ten-year renovation the hotel is back on top again. According to its Web site, "The Biltmore will introduce a brand new, 12,000 sq. ft. destination Spa on the seventh floor of the hotel. Featuring spectacular views of surrounding Coral Gables, the Biltmore Spa will offer a luxurious and sophisticated setting for state-of-the-art treatments and services. Treatments will also be available in the hotel's soon-to-be refurbished, private poolside cabanas." The Biltmore has a four-star, four-diamond rating and rooms go for $350 per night. Here's something else that's rich—Congress gave the hotel $775,000 as part of a program to fund projects to provide economic opportunity in areas of the country with populations with low or moderate incomes. But Coral Gable's per capita income (at $46,000) is neither low nor moderate—it's actually 19.6 percent greater than the national average ($37,000). The name of the earmarked money for Biltmore should have been called Bilk-more because Congress keeps bilking more and more of our money.

"When I picked the Secretary of Education I wanted somebody who knew something about public education."

—*George W. Bush, Washington, D.C., April 30, 2003*

PAPER DOESN'T GROW ON TREES, YOU KNOW—WELL, SORT OF ...

What is Appleton, Wisconsin, known for? Cheese? Rabid football fans? No, it's the Paper Industry International Hall of Fame. At least Representative Mark Green (R-Wisconsin) knows about it. According to the Hall of Fame's Web site, "Any individual, living or deceased, who has pioneered and/or uniquely helped the world's paper industry flourish, is eligible for induction into the Paper Industry International Hall of Fame."

Congress gave this important Hall of Fame $70,000 in 2005 and for that they should be inducted, because Congress has helped the world's paper industry flourish with the huge amount of money they use (on worthless projects I might add).

"Free societies are hopeful societies. And free societies will be allies against these hateful few who have no conscience, who kill at the whim of a hat."
—*George W. Bush, Washington, D.C., September 17, 2004*

DON'T HAVE A COW, MAN

Got milk? Got $2 billion in milk? Well, the U.S. Government does. The Milk Income Loss Contract is a $2 billion annual program used to subsidize dairy farmers when milk prices drop. In its first month, October 2003, MILC (I know it's a cute acronym) paid out nearly $500 million in subsidies, far above what was originally estimated. In addition to MILC is the $8 million given to the U.S. Dairy Industry to become more competitive and to keep the industry stable and growing. But the U.S. Dairy Industry doesn't need any growth hormones—it's already a $43 billion industry.

We taxpayers aren't the only ones getting milked.

"I'm honored to, uhh, shake the hand—
of a brave Iraqi citizen who had his hand cut off by Saddam
Hussein. Ummm, I'm with six other Iraqi citizens, as well,
who suffered the same fate. Uhh, they are examples of
the —brutality, uhh, of the tyrant."
—*George W. Bush, Washington, D.C., May 25, 2004*

WHEN I SAY JUMP, YOU JUMP

QUESTION: If George W. Bush has a second term, you're going to stick around for another four years?

SECOND REPORTER: He's thinking about it.

SECRETARY RUMSFELD: I didn't hear the question.

QUESTION: Oh, I'm sorry.

SECRETARY RUMSFELD: No, I did hear it, but I didn't hear it.

QUESTION: [Laughter] Oh, okay. All right. Not actually answering that one.

SECRETARY RUMSFELD: I don't know. You know, those are the kinds of things that you think about down the road. Adlai Stevenson, my former governor in Illinois, had this quote he said, "I'll jump off that bridge when I get to it."

QUESTION: [Laughs] That's very funny. That's a good plan for you, sir.

—*Secretary of Defense Donald Rumsfeld, interview with WAPI-AM Radio, Richard Dixon, Birmingham, Alabama, September 28, 2004*

"The enemy understands a free Iraq will be a major defeat in their ideology of hatred. That's why they're fighting so vociferously."

—*George W. Bush, First Presidential Debate, Coral Gables, Florida, September 30, 2004*

SO, IN OTHER WORDS OUR ENEMY IS FIGHTING REALLY LOUDLY?

A REAL GRIND

Next time you go into a Starbucks and burn up the majority of a twenty-dollar bill on a cup of coffee and a sweet roll you might wonder—why did Congress give the International Coffee Organization $500,000 in 2005? The rationale is the coffee industry took a turn for the worse in 2002 when the market was flooded with cheaper product. So not only are you paying a premium price for a cup of coffee, the industry that's charging you that much is on the government dole. The coffee industry filters out about $70 billion in annual sales—how's that for leaving a bad taste in your mouth.

"By making the right choices, we can make the right choice for our future."
—*George W. Bush, Dallas, Texas, July 18, 2003*

SPACE, THE FINAL FRONTIER

The High Frequency Active Auroral Research Project (HAARP), championed by legendary pork-barreler, Ted Stevens (R-Alaska), is a boondoggle to end all boondoggles. Until recently, HAARP was touted as a means of sucking energy from the aurora borealis, but since the creation of the Department of Homeland Security, HAARP is now configured to heat up the ionosphere for military communications. In Fiscal Year 2005 alone, this project received $5 million of our money and since its inception, the project has received more than $95 million. From 1997 to 2004, Stevens held the position of Chairman of the Senate Appropriations Committee. Now that he's Chairman of the Defense Appropriations Subcommittee, HAARP recently changed its standing to a military program, too.

"We will make sure our troops have all that is necessary to complete their missions. That's why I went to the Congress last September and proposed fundamental— supplemental funding, which is money for armor and body parts and ammunition and fuel."

—*George W. Bush, Erie, Pennsylvania, September 4, 2004*

A PIG IN A POKE

So far this book has explained some of the ridiculous programs on which Congress is wasting our money. Now let's look at the states whose representatives really know how to bring home the bacon. In 2004, the watchdog organization Citizens Against Government Waste noted that Alaska, with one of the smallest populations in the United States, receives, per capita, the most pork-barrel money from the United States government. With a population of 648,818, Alaska received $524,329,000 from the federal government: that translates to $808.13 for every man, woman, and child living in Alaska. The second runner-up was Hawaii with $392.92 per person ($494,136,000 with a population of 1,257,608). By contrast, California, the most heavily populated state with 35,484,453 (nearly fifty-five times more residents than Alaska) received $642,854,000 that translates to $18.12 per person. It's not a matter of need, it's a matter of who's in charge of doling out the money. Who are the two most powerful senators on the appropriations subcommittee? Ted Stevens, Republican senator from Alaska, and Daniel Inouye, Democrat senator from Hawaii.

———————•———————

"You'll hear, we're going to spend—
the government is going to spend the government
money here, and the government is going to spend
the government here."

—*George W. Bush, Trenton, New Jersey,*
September 23, 2002

"I HOPE YOU LEAVE HERE AND WALK OUT AND SAY,

'WHAT DID HE SAY?'"

—*George W. Bush, Beaverton, Oregon, August 13, 2004*